The Promise of
Easter

D1632968

C015500433

Published by
The Bible Reading Fellowship
15 The Chambers, Vineyard
Abingdon OX14 3FE
United Kingdom
Tel: +44 (0)1865 319700
Email: enquiries@brf.org.uk
Website: www.brf.org.uk
BRF is a Registered Charity

ISBN 978 1 84101 788 4

First published 2010
10 9 8 7 6 5 4 3 2 1 0

Acknowledgments
Unless otherwise stated, scripture quotations are taken from the Holy Bible,
New International Version, copyright © 1973, 1978, 1984 by International
Bible Society, and are used by permission of Hodder & Stoughton
Publishers, a member of the Hachette Livre UK Group. All rights reserved.
'NIV' is a registered trademark of International Bible Society. UK trademark
number 1448790.

Scriptures taken from The Revised Standard Version of the Bible, copyright
© 1946, 1952, 1971 by the Division of Christian Education of the National
Council of the Churches of Christ in the United States of America, are used
by permission. All rights reserved.

A catalogue record for this book is available from the British Library

Printed in Great Britain by CPI Bookmarque, Croydon

The Promise of *Easter*

30 reflections for the season of Lent

Fleur Dorrell

Contents

Beginnings

Here are 30 meditations for you to read throughout Lent.

You may wish to light a candle or use a short stilling exercise to help you relax and centre yourself on God. Try the following:

- Sit in a comfortable position with as few distractions as possible.
- Slowly begin to listen to the silence.
- Without changing your breathing at all, notice your breath gently entering your body and leaving it. In your mind's eye, scan your body and notice how it feels. Don't do anything unless you want to; just be aware of how you feel in this silence.
- Now take a slightly longer breath in and out. Enjoy the feeling of breathing.
- Feel more relaxed and at peace with yourself.

Ask God for what you desire at this time. When you are ready, whether alone or in a group, read the day's Bible passage silently and slowly. Take time to hear God speaking through his word.

The Bible passages are taken from the New International Version but you may like to compare other translations and versions.

Each Bible passage is followed by a commentary and questions and exercises to help you reflect personally.

- What is God saying to you today through this text?
- Be there with God and for God; really hunger for God.
- Listen to what God is saying to you in the depths of your heart.

Each meditation concludes with a prayer and a final thought for you to take away.

May this Easter journey illuminate your soul.

Images

Nature's passion for Lent and Easter

Lent is the most poignant time of year for Christians, and nature agrees with us as it offers us the passion flower (pictured on the cover of this book).

This plant (native to the tropical Americas) is so called because it reveals the complexity of Christ's sufferings. Its symbolism was first captured by the Mexican friar Emmanuel de Villegas, who reported it, with drawings, in 1610. Passion flower symbolism includes:

- The spiralled tendrils: the lash of Christ's scourging
- The central flower column: the pillar of the scourging
- The 72 radial filaments: the crown of thorns
- The top three stigma: three nails
- The lower five anthers: five wounds
- The style: the sponge moistening Christ's lips with vinegar
- The leaves (some species): the head of the centurion's spear
- The red stains: drops of Christ's blood
- The round fruit: the world that Christ came to save
- The fragrance: the spices prepared by the women

You may wish to look at some other pictures that, throughout history, have interpreted our Easter journey. There are links to all of these pictures on our website at www.brfonline.org.uk/the-promise-of-easter, but the URLs are provided below so you can type in the addresses directly if you prefer.

Holiness
Ecce Ancilla Domini! (The Annunciation), Dante Gabriel Rossetti.
www.tate.org.uk/servlet/ViewWork?workid=12768

Relationship
The Good Samaritan, Vincent Van Gogh.
www.artbible.info/art/large/595.html

Forgiveness
The Return of the Prodigal Son, Rembrandt van Rijn.
www.hermitagemuseum.org (search 'Return of the Prodigal Son')

Sacrifice
The Shadow of Death, William Holman Hunt.
www.manchestergalleries.org/the-collections/search-the-collection (enter 'The shadow of death')

Hope
The Baptism of Christ, Piero della Francesca.
www.nationalgallery.org.uk (search 'Baptism of Christ')

Love
Jesus Washing Peter's Feet, Ford Madox Brown.
www.tate.org.uk/servlet/ViewWork?workid=1581

The Supper at Emmaus, Michelangelo Merisi da Caravaggio.
www.nationalgallery.org.uk (search 'Supper at Emmaus')

Introduction

Lent is not a time of waiting so much as accompanying. During Lent we are accompanying Christ in a unique way, on a journey that will lead to his death entirely for our sake, bringing God's humanity in touch with our humanity. Although we are spared all of his agony, it is a time for us to pause and reflect, to pray and, above all, stay very close to Jesus. On this journey towards wholeness and salvation through Christ, we are given plenty of opportunities to understand his loving purpose.

By reading the Bible each day during Lent and drawing on texts from both the Old and the New Testaments, we are shown a spiritual map. This map can deepen our faith and give us new insights into the most remarkable events of all time. This map leads us to Christ, but the journey is far from easy; it is a lifetime's work, involving pain and sorrow as well as joy and infinite love. So we must not despair; we must not give up when it seems impossible, because without our own inevitable crosses we cannot imagine Christ's greater suffering. We are not alone; we are not abandoned for ever. Glory will come at the end, and, although we cannot really comprehend Christ's resurrection, we firmly believe in its power. Christ conquered death and rose to new life. Easter gives us hope to bring this new life into our hearts.

On this journey we will be exploring six aspects of God's revelation to us through a variety of women, men and biblical events. These six aspects are holiness, relationship, forgiveness, sacrifice, hope and love. They are crucial to Christ's suffering, death and resurrection; they also shape our own humanity if we are to serve God. Taking each one in turn, we will think about how it enables us to accompany Christ on the journey, and to make sense of the many Bible stories that predict and show the shape of Jesus' mission on earth.

The passages I have chosen reflect the complexity of human nature as well as our profound desire and need to follow God. The paths that the people of long ago trod, the lives they led, the hand of God in their world—all these become richer in the context of the Messiah's purpose. From the poor to the wealthy, the forgotten to the acclaimed, the uneducated to the wise—woman, child or man, priest, prophet, king or queen—these characters can be found in today's world, just as they were 2000 years ago. Thus the power of God can work marvels today just as it did then. Despite the cynicism in our world, which discourages us from believing in miracles and encourages our fear of anything greater than our own arrogance, the awesome acts of God defy human limitation. If they didn't, they would not come from God.

So may this Lenten season ground us in reality—reality that acknowledges humanity, its mess and violence, ambition and greed, power and death, yet also contains an understanding of divine beauty, peace, love and truth. A reality that stretches way back to our ancestors and the stirrings of creation, that gives us generous glimpses of the extraordinary and new ways that God works to open the doors to our souls. A reality that always leads us to Christ.

God's message is for all time, not just Lent, yet during this season we are called in a special way to follow him, to take up our cross, to enter into the mysteries of the passion and the mind of Christ. Most of all, we are asked to show the world pure love.

It was out of love that God gave us his only Son;
it was out of love that Christ laid down his life for us;
it was out of love that Christ called us to him;
it was out of love that Jesus came quietly from the tomb.
Jesus is this love.

May we rise with Christ on Easter Sunday and go forth in his love.

Holiness

You are to gather up the joys and sorrows, the struggles, the beauty, love, dreams and hopes of every hour that they may be consecrated at the altar of daily life.

SR MACRINA WIEDERKEHR OSB, FROM *A TREE FULL OF ANGELS: SEEING THE HOLY IN THE ORDINARY* (HARPERCOLLINS, 1988)

In the Old Testament, the concept of holiness is understood primarily as something that describes the majestic, glorious, invisible God (see Exodus 15:11; Psalm 29:2), but his holiness may also be extended to places, objects and divinely elected people (Exodus 3:5; 22:31; 29:37). It is significant that all the biblical places, encounters and objects that were described as holy and sacred were marked out for their manifestations of the divine presence. Where God dwelt, holiness dwelt; and, by implication, where God was not, holiness was not. God's relationship towards his chosen people, described as a holy nation (Exodus 19:6; Deuteronomy 7:6), was also marked out by his everlasting covenant with them and his demand for their worship of him alone (Exodus 20:1–3). At this point, then, holiness is identified as separation from other nations and as relationship with the Divine.

In the Old Testament, the greatest emphasis on

holiness was found first in its relation to ceremonial and ritual activities. With the emergence of the later prophets, such as Isaiah, Jeremiah and Ezekiel, and the rise of Wisdom literature (such as is found in the books of Proverbs and Ecclesiastes), the term 'holiness' became more abstract, but was still waiting to be born in the coming Messiah. Jesus both models holiness and is the door to holiness—and we are invited in.

In the New Testament, we find Jesus depicted by the Gospel writers as taking the idea of holiness one stage further, by saying that holiness is no longer to be found only in buildings, places, objects, rituals and prescribed Law, but in the individual person, in one's heart. The Gospel writers used the word 'heart' in this context to represent the whole person, rather as we do today. The heart was the seat of the emotions and appetites, and included intellectual and moral faculties. Thus the experience of the way holiness is defined and practised shifts from being centred predominantly outside the body to being placed firmly within it.

Jesus frequently castigated the religious leaders of his time precisely because they had lost this intrinsic meaning of holiness in the ways they interpreted the Law. They had developed and perpetuated an elaborate system of rules regarding holiness that was designed exclusively to separate them from the rest of the people. Indeed, the very word 'Pharisee' meant separation—a person who was set apart for a life of purity. Yet, through Christ, holiness is no longer something that separates God from humanity; no longer do holy things or places divide the Creator from

Moses on holy ground

Now Moses was tending the flock of Jethro his father-in-law, the priest of Midian, and he led the flock to the far side of the desert and came to Horeb, the mountain of God. There the angel of the Lord appeared to him in flames of fire from within a bush. Moses saw that though the bush was on fire it did not burn up. So Moses thought, 'I will go over and see this strange sight—why the bush does not burn up.' When the Lord saw that he had gone over to look, God called to him from within the bush, 'Moses, Moses!' And Moses said, 'Here I am.' 'Do not come any closer,' God said. 'Take off your sandals, for the place where you are standing is holy ground.' Then he said, 'I am the God of your father, the God of Abraham, the God of Isaac and the God of Jacob.' At this, Moses hid his face, because he was afraid to look at God.

EXODUS 3:1–6

First we read that Moses was curious: it was his curiosity and a mysterious fascination that led him to go and look at the burning bush. There always have been plenty of plants in deserts that can ignite spontaneously but are rapidly destroyed by their own combustion. A bush that burned without being consumed was indeed a strange phenomenon. So not only was this sight peculiar, but also a voice appeared out of the bush, and it was God's voice. Yet we notice that God did not speak to Moses until he had Moses' attention—until Moses had physically gone over to the bush. Often God's words do not touch our hearts and minds in the way that we might expect because we do not always give them our full attention. Here is a call to see and hear God differently.

Here we have a thorn-bush (the original Hebrew word comes from the word 'to prick'—thus a 'thorn-bush or bramble'—and is also a Hebrew pun on a similar word for Sinai). This image is a reminder of the curse of Adam in Genesis 3:18, when he was doomed to bring forth thorns and thistles from the earth. In this moment the 'curse' is burnt (a picture of judgment) without being consumed; therefore, it is a picture of God's mercy and grace. The thorn-bush may also be symbolic for Israel in other respects. As the thorn-bush is the lowliest of all species of trees, so the nation in exile is the lowliest compared with all other nations. That is why Moses received his calling from the bush, to deliver the Hebrew people from their suffering and exile in Egypt.

Moses realises that it is God who is calling him but, as yet, God cannot reveal himself directly. God therefore asks Moses to take off his shoes and stand at a distance from the bush, from him. 'Do not come any closer' has the literal sense of 'Stop coming nearer'. Moses was clearly on his way to a thorough examination of this bush when God stopped him short. God explains that the bush and its surroundings are holy ground: Moses experiences this holiness as separate from him but connected to his faith, because God declares his relationship to the patriarchs. This reminds Moses that God is the God of the covenant with Israel. This is not an encounter between a 'new God' and Moses, but the same God who called Abraham, Isaac and Jacob. (Later, however, in Exodus 3:14, Moses will ask God to tell him his name and will be given the more mysterious answer, 'I am who I am.')

Moses is commanded to show reverence for God's presence: 'Take off your sandals'. Removing the sandals implied humility, because the poorest people had no shoes, and servants usually went barefoot. It also implied a recognition of the immediate presence of God. In many cultures, we take off our shoes when we enter religious buildings or someone's house, and now Moses is in God's 'house', a place of his immediate presence. Hiding his face from God was also a natural reaction. In Exodus 33:20, God says, 'You cannot see my face, for no one may see me and live'. To look directly at God would require enormous, not to say reckless, confidence in one's own goodness, and Moses was just as human as we are.

The burning bush captured Moses' attention but it changed nothing until he received the word of God there, calling him by name. Even though Moses was then an obscure shepherd on the far side of the desert, God knew who he was, and Moses was significant to God.

❖

Spiritual exercise

❖ Imagine you are seeing the strange phenomenon of the burning bush. What is it that draws you to this bush? Is it pure curiosity or something else? What colours do you see in the flames and how does the heat feel across your face?

❖ When you hear God's voice, what is its tone? Will you also want to cover your face?

❖ What does this passage reveal to you about your image of God?

Prayer

Holy, holy, holy Lord,
God of majesty and might,
God of burning bushes
and sacred ground.
Come to me again this Lent.
Come as fire and grace,
and burn brightly within my heart.
Amen

Reflection

Holy ground is wherever we encounter God. It can be a physical place or a spiritual state. Whatever or wherever it is for you, may you hear God calling you this Lent.

Elijah and gentleness

There he went into a cave and spent the night. And the word of the Lord came to him: 'What are you doing here, Elijah?' He replied, 'I have been very zealous for the Lord God Almighty...' The Lord said, 'Go out and stand on the mountain in the presence of the Lord, for the Lord is about to pass by.' Then a great and powerful wind tore the mountains apart and shattered the rocks before the Lord, but the Lord was not in the wind. After the wind there was an earthquake, but the Lord was not in the earthquake. After the earthquake came a fire, but the Lord was not in the fire. And after the fire came a gentle whisper. When Elijah heard it, he pulled his cloak over his face and went out and stood at the mouth of the cave.

1 KINGS 19:9–13A (ABRIDGED)

Elijah is not what anyone would consider a reserved prophet. We do not expect to see him engaged in lengthy silence and stillness. This fire-breathing prophet is not the quiet type. Yet Elijah's experience of God is described as the opposite of that of Moses in some aspects: having heard, seen and felt a thunderstorm, earthquake and fire, Elijah recognises, hears and feels God only in the gentle breeze. Why might this be? Perhaps the biblical writers wanted to distinguish their God from the rival gods of their time, who were often

21

associated with power over natural phenomena. In order for Elijah to recognise God separately from these gods, God needed to be revealed with the opposite characteristics.

Nevertheless, natural phenomena are present in Elijah's encounter with God, as well as in Moses' meeting at the burning bush. The biblical writers sought to show that not only could humanity be changed through an experience of holiness but also through the physical world.

When Elijah prays for the rains to stay away, they do, and when he prays for them to return, they do (1 Kings 17:1–4; 18:41–45). When he prays, people are healed and miracles happen (17:8–24). Elijah has stood before kings and is not afraid, yet this great man of faith finds himself in the desert, alone, burnt out and faithless. He cries out to God just to kill him now, please (19:1–8). Instead, God gives Elijah food and drink, and sends him off to Mount Horeb (the same mountain on which Moses saw the burning bush), where he climbs into a cave for warmth and shelter. God asks him, 'What are you doing here, Elijah?' Elijah tells him that he has worked hard for God, but has failed. The enemies—Ahab, Jezebel and her Baal worshippers—have killed all of God's people. He is the only one left and they are pursuing him now.

God asks him to go and watch at the cave's mouth. Elijah sees a violent storm tearing rocks out of the earth: this is the kind of man Elijah is, obeying the wild wind of God's power. But God is not in the wind. Then Elijah sees an earthquake. Like an earthquake, Elijah is always shaking things up, disturbing the status quo, but God is not in the earthquake either. The prophet of fire then sees the fire: he is the one who called down fire from heaven (1 Kings 18:36–38), the one who will disappear into the heavens in a chariot of fire (2 Kings 2:11). Yet God is not in the fire either. In a still small whisper, Elijah finally hears God. He tells Elijah to go from Horeb and anoint Elisha, Jehu and Hazael, men who would together complete the work that he had begun.

As Elijah becomes a temporary caveman, God gently rebukes him for abandoning his prophetic role. A prophet's work is among the people, not hidden away in a dark remote place. Elijah stands face to face with three natural disasters, but God is not in any of them. Once he realises that God is in the breeze, he covers his face because he knows, as God had told Moses, that no one can see God's face and live. The still, calm presence of God is more dangerous and powerful than all the natural disasters of earth put together. To encounter God is to experience the most awesome phenomenon in the universe.

Spiritual exercise

❖ Think about the elements that are working in this passage—a storm, fire, earthquake and gentle breeze. What do they evoke for you?

❖ Can you remember any storms or fires in your own life?
❖ Reflect on a time when you were in the presence of God—recall this moment now. What does God's gentle whisper say to you today about God?

Prayer

Holy, holy, holy Lord,
in the midst of my life—
the storms that rise up,
the earthquakes that shatter my stability
and the fires that burn long into the night—
may I be sensitive to your still, calm voice.
Clothe me in gentleness as you pass by my side.
Amen

Reflection

God's gentleness is as powerful as his fire, wind and earthquakes. This Lent, seek God in his gentleness and be gentle with the people around you.

Angel's wings

In the sixth month, God sent the angel Gabriel to Nazareth, a town in Galilee, to a virgin pledged to be married to a man named Joseph, a descendant of David. The virgin's name was Mary. The angel went to her and said, 'Greetings, you who are highly favoured! The Lord is with you.' Mary was greatly troubled at his words and wondered what kind of greeting this might be. But the angel said to her, 'Do not be afraid, Mary, you have found favour with God. You will be with child and give birth to a son, and you are to give him the name of Jesus. He will be great and will be called the Son of the Most High. The Lord God will give him the throne of his father David, and he will reign over the house of Jacob for ever; his kingdom will never end.' 'How will this be,' Mary asked the angel, 'since I am a virgin?' The angel answered, 'The Holy Spirit will come upon you, and the power of the Most High will overshadow you. So the holy one to be born will be called the Son of God.'

LUKE 1:26–35

Mary's encounter with holiness is different from Moses' and Elijah's because Mary becomes the sacred place herself. She is the holy ground where God's presence will dwell; she is the instrument of the Messiah's birth. Yet, like the two prophets, Mary's experience of holiness involves the idea of a covering or concealment before God, as Jesus would remain hidden in her womb for nine months. Just as in the case of John the Baptist, God himself names the child.

Mary's virginity naturally makes her question the angel's announcement that she will soon conceive a son. Similarly, Zechariah knows his wife Elizabeth's old age, which makes him question Gabriel's news of John's birth (see vv. 13–18). Both Mary and Zechariah ask for an explanation of how such a miraculous birth will be possible, yet the angel responds to them in very different ways.

Gabriel strikes Zechariah mute because he has not believed the angel's words. He remains mute until the day of his son's circumcision, when he puts his trust in God by writing down that he agrees for Elizabeth to call their son John, as ordained by God, even though none of their family bears that name. The sign has been reversed and Zechariah is allowed to speak again. Zechariah blesses God in his beautiful prayer, which the church knows as the Benedictus (Luke 1:68–79).

By contrast, in Mary's encounter with the angel, she is not rebuked at all. Gabriel says nothing about her lack of faith, because her simple and honest question is not about her faith or lack of it, so much as about her current physical status. Whether or not Mary is asking for a sign, Gabriel gives her one in verses 36–38: the miraculous conception of her cousin Elizabeth's child is the sign that Gabriel's promise to Mary will indeed come true.

The divine nature of Jesus existed from eternity; the

human nature of Jesus did not. When the incarnation occurred, each of the divine and the human natures shared in the qualities of the other nature, because they were united in the one person of Christ. When Jesus became human he had both the earthly characteristics of a baby who needs its parents' care and the divine characteristics of a person with a particular mission to fulfil, as determined by his Father in heaven. This dynamic of who Jesus is remains a crucial part of our faith, and is difficult to understand—but this is why Gabriel describes Jesus as a 'holy' child. Jesus will be holy because he will be conceived by the Holy Spirit; he will be God-made-man and therefore without sin.

Mary's 'yes' to God is a wonderful expression of faith. In her words, Mary demonstrates that she firmly believes that God's promise through Gabriel will indeed be fulfilled. Her faith is necessary to the incarnation, but it is also a statement of willing submission to God's promise for her, as are all statements of faith. She openly accepts God's plan for her life, including all the potential inconveniences and risks involved. These inconveniences included the possibility that Joseph would divorce her, that her reputation would be destroyed, and that even if Joseph believed her, their life would be very different from anything she had previously imagined or planned. Yet Mary still says 'yes' to God in total faith and surrender.

❖

Spiritual exercise

❖ Imagine what it must have been like for Mary on an ordinary day in Nazareth, hearing this news without any warning. Picture how Mary must have felt on being told she would be the Messiah's mother.

❖ When you reflect on Mary's calling, which words strike you most? What do Gabriel's words reveal to you about your own faith?

Prayer

Holy, holy, holy Lord,
throughout the ages men and women
have followed you in faith,
and you call me once more
to say 'yes' to you—no matter the risks to myself.
Give me courage when I feel hesitant
to believe that it is you whom I follow.
Amen

Reflection

'Do not be afraid,' says Gabriel; yet how often do we fear the known and the unknown? This Lent, ask God to help you overcome one of your fears with peace.

Death tearing

At that moment the curtain of the temple was torn in two from top to bottom. The earth shook and the rocks split. The tombs broke open and the bodies of many holy people who had died were raised to life.
MATTHEW 27:51–52

The curtain of the temple was torn in two from top to bottom. And when the centurion, who stood there in front of Jesus, heard his cry and saw how he died, he said, 'Surely this man was the Son of God!'
MARK 15:38–39

It was about the sixth hour, and darkness came over the whole land until the ninth hour, for the sun stopped shining. And the curtain of the temple was torn in two. Jesus called out with a loud voice, 'Father, into your hands I commit my spirit.' When he had said this, he breathed his last.
LUKE 23:44–46

It is intriguing that the brief mention of the temple curtain's tearing at the moment of Christ's death in the Synoptic Gospels is interpreted by many scholars to have transformed the entire Old Testament concept of holiness. The tearing of this one curtain symbolised that access to the holy presence of God through Jesus was now available to everyone. If this were not true, then why did three of the Gospel writers mention such a specific detail?

Exodus 26:31–35 recounts the original making of a curtain for the tabernacle, to conceal the ark of the covenant from public view. In the temple at the time of Jesus, very few people would have known where the curtain hung: its precise location would have been known only to the high priest, as it separated the Holy of Holies from the Holy Place and the rest of the temple. The high priest alone entered the Holy of Holies, once a year, to pray and ask for the nation's sins to be forgiven. The tearing of the curtain would have been meaningless unless its symbolic value represented something greater than its presence. By including this detail, the Gospel writers wanted to demonstrate that the unapproachable had now become approachable. It was a reversal of the divine encounters of Moses and Elijah, as they were asked to stand back and hide their faces; now there was permission for a more direct understanding and experience of holiness.

The curtain of the temple was very high and immensely thick. We notice that it was torn from top to bottom rather than from the bottom upwards. This was not the work of human hands, because that would have meant tearing it from the bottom. It was the work of God: the tearing had been done from heaven to earth. God's presence was no longer confined to the Holy of Holies; he would never again dwell in a temple made with hands. God had fulfilled everything he wanted to achieve with the temple, its religious system and its worship. Later, in AD70, the temple and the city of Jerusalem itself were 'left desolate' (see Matthew 23:38), destroyed by the Romans. Christ's coming brought the new covenant, which established a new relationship with all people, in all times and all places.

Spiritual exercise

❖ What differences and similarities do you notice in the accounts of the tearing of the curtain? What do they reveal to you about your understanding of God?

❖ Are there any barriers in your own church that prevent people from finding God? How can you help people to see God?

Prayer

Holy, holy, holy Lord,
you tore the temple curtain
that had separated us from you for so long.
So now, as I enter your presence,
may I never be torn apart by doubts or fears
that I am unworthy to draw near to you. Amen

Reflection

Jesus Christ has removed the barriers between God and humanity. This Lent, let us remove any barriers that we have placed between ourselves and God.

Blessed is the King

After Jesus had said this, he went on ahead, going up to Jerusalem. As he approached Bethphage and Bethany at the hill called the Mount of Olives, he sent two of his disciples, saying to them, 'Go to the village ahead of you, and as you enter it, you will find a colt tied there, which no one has ever ridden. Untie it and bring it here. If anyone asks you, "Why are you untying it?" tell him, "The Lord needs it."' ... They brought it to Jesus, threw their cloaks on the colt and put Jesus on it. As he went along, people spread their cloaks on the road. When he came near the place where the road goes down the Mount of Olives, the whole crowd of disciples began joyfully to praise God in loud voices for all the miracles they had seen: 'Blessed is the king who comes in the name of the Lord!' 'Peace in heaven and glory in the highest!'

LUKE 19:28–31, 35–38

Jesus and his followers probably came by foot all the way from Galilee, but for the last two miles he wanted to ride a donkey. In this, Jesus was deliberately acting out the prophecies of Isaiah 62:11 and Zechariah 9:9. The crowds lined the street, shouting with praise in the words of Psalm 118:25–26, and placed palm branches and robes in front of Jesus. This was highly disturbing to the religious leaders who were jealous of him. They demanded that Jesus silence the crowd, but he responded that even if the crowd were silent, the stones would cry out (v. 40).

One of the reasons why Jesus had been silent about his identity during his earlier ministry, and had urged his disciples to tell no one that he was the Messiah, was that he did not want to encourage messianic expectations that were nationalistic and political in nature and thus contrary to his own understanding of a suffering messiahship. As he was about to enter Jerusalem and face rejection, hostility, humiliation and death, the possibility of misunderstanding his messianic nature was no longer an issue. The time of Jesus' suffering and death were drawing nearer, so he could expressly demonstrate that he indeed was the Messiah.

The events of the next week would change the world for ever. Jesus entered Jerusalem and the crowd welcomed him as a king. By the end of the week, they were demanding his death. His disciples and followers abandoned him in fear. Most of his close friends did not really understand the events of Palm Sunday and Holy Week until after Jesus had risen from the dead. They had all expected Jesus to be an earthly king, but God gave them someone and something so much more valuable—an open door into a kingdom without end.

The acclamation of the crowd of disciples, 'Blessed is the king who comes in the name of the Lord', was the usual greeting for Passover pilgrims entering Jerusalem, except that the word 'king' has been added. What is so intriguing about this event is that Luke wants us to understand it as a normal pilgrimage to Jerusalem for an annual celebration that commemorated the exodus event. Yet within the story there are clear hints that this is not a normal event at all. This is a royal visit to a royal city.

Spiritual exercise

❖ Imagine you are in this story; can you identify with one of the people involved?
❖ Take time to see the places, the people and the mood. What kind of day is it? Imagine the sounds, colours and smells if that helps the scene to become present to you.
❖ What would you like to ask or say to Jesus in this moment of his mission?

Prayer

Holy, holy, holy Lord,
your mother rode a donkey before your birth;
now you ride a colt before your death.
I cry out to you in love as I sing:
'Blessed is your name in all the world—
my royal Saviour, my King of kings.' Amen

Reflection

A colt was untied and cloaks were laid down for our Messiah. This Lent, may we untie everything that binds us and lay down our cloaks in the path of Christ.

Relationship

*The whole idea of compassion is based on a keen aware-
ness of the interdependence of all these living beings,
which are all part of one another, and all involved in
one another.*

THOMAS MERTON (1915–1968), DURING A CONFERENCE ON EAST–WEST
MONASTIC DIALOGUE, JUST TWO HOURS BEFORE HIS DEATH

Relationship is the art of living together, whether it is
a relationship between two people, family members, a
large group or a global community. For us as Christians,
relationships are fundamentally about how we stand
before God. Relationships affect every aspect of our
lives and the Bible is our model for understanding their
complexity.

For the people of ancient Israel, the home was the
first place for the formation of relationships. The home
was central to the nurturing of beliefs and traditions,
maintaining links between faith and ethnicity and,
therefore, identity. Next to the home came the tribe,
which was fiercely protected and sustained. Once God
had made his covenant with Israel, after the exodus, the
idea of the chosen nation became paramount. Within
this covenantal relationship, the people expressed their
faith in the one God, Yahweh. Throughout Old Testa-

ment times, the promise of the Messiah comforted and inspired those who remained faithful to the covenant, so when Jesus was born it should have been obvious how to respond to him. Yet Jesus' birth contradicted many of their illusions about kingship and salvation, so he was not widely recognised or affirmed.

One of the aspects of Jesus' ministry that challenged the social order was that of service. He exemplified the role of servant to others, but this was a very hard lesson for the people of Israel to understand. Their entire lives had been patterned on unequal relationships with those who oppressed them, whether in the family or tribe or among other nations. So when Jesus spoke about the kingdom of God and how it affected relationships— the last being first, and the first being last (Matthew 20:16)—he was speaking to people who had to turn their minds and hearts upside down to understand his message.

For Jesus, spiritual transformation in the minds and hearts of his hearers also meant a direct transformation of society. He wanted to change the way relationships were organised and lived out, so he always accompanied his teaching with public actions of justice and equality. Jesus' command to love, which was his most important value (Matthew 22:36–40), was also a call to action, a disturbing wake-up call for justice to operate in society, a call that clearly threatened many individual interests and political agendas.

In order to share his message, Jesus always took people as he found them, and made his teachings and parables relevant to their lives. He used their personal situations and stories to illustrate his truths and values. The word 'parable' is derived from the Greek *parabole*, meaning 'placing two things side by side for the sake of comparison'. In Hebrew, the word is *mashal*, meaning a story told by a rabbi to make his teaching clear and intelligible. Parables were a very common tool for explaining a truth, and Jesus made full use of them.

Jesus also drew heavily on the Old Testament scriptures, frequently quoting from them or referring to them in context when he was making a specific point. He never simply repeated the scriptures but developed the texts with which Jewish people would have been familiar, to draw out new levels of understanding. Jesus quoted from many different Old Testament books and, like all the Jews of the first century, divided the Old Testament into three sections: the Law, the Prophets and the Psalms. Jesus said, 'This is what I told you while I was still with you: everything must be fulfilled that is written about me in the Law of Moses, the Prophets and the Psalms' (Luke 24:44). He quoted from the scriptures to explain what he was doing, to rebuke those who were disobedient and to show how his actions and mission were in accordance with biblical prophecies and teachings. Crucially, he revealed deeper meaning in the scriptures so that the people were not narrowly bound by them but were liberated through their message.

Jesus would ask people to do something practical with what he had taught them. By applying what they had learnt, his listeners could make connections between understanding and doing. They could live

Two nations

Isaac prayed to the Lord on behalf of his wife, because she was barren. The Lord answered his prayer, and his wife Rebekah became pregnant. The babies jostled each other within her, and she said, 'Why is this happening to me?' So she went to inquire of the Lord. The Lord said to her, 'Two nations are in your womb, and two peoples from within you will be separated; one people will be stronger than the other, and the older will serve the younger.' When the time came for her to give birth, there were twin boys in her womb. The first to come out was red, and his whole body was like a hairy garment; so they named him Esau. After this, his brother came out, with his hand grasping Esau's heel; so he was named Jacob… Isaac, who had a taste for wild game, loved Esau, but Rebekah loved Jacob.
GENESIS 25:21–26A, 28

In all his work of creation, God knows the end, the final outcome, from the very beginning. He knew, before Jacob and Esau were born, exactly what type of personalities they would manifest as they grew up. God knew that Esau would disobey him.

God answered the longings of Rebekah, who had feared that she would never have a child—but notice that she finally conceived through the intercession of Isaac, and not through her own prayers. This is important because it symbolises the power of God to act throughout Abraham's lineage (Abraham being the father of Isaac).

Rebekah's pregnancy is interpreted as a struggle, not just between the twin boys in her womb but between the two nations that these boys would come to represent: Israel and Edom. God tells Rebekah that, contrary to Israelite custom, the older boy will serve his younger brother: the future history of these two sons is foretold before they are born. Esau is so named because of a play on the Hebrew words 'red' and 'hairy', while the root of Jacob's name means 'heel-gripper' or 'heel-grabber' because he held on to Esau's foot as they were being born. Both these names are loaded against Esau and will burden him all his life, while Jacob's innately slippery character and subsequent deceitfulness are also revealed as their story unfolds.

Isaac loved Esau better than Jacob, because Esau provided him with meat. He was proud of his bold, spirited son who excelled in hunting (v. 27). Rebekah preferred Jacob because he was more domesticated and, presumably, therefore better able to please his mother. Did Rebekah tell Jacob of the prophecy, given before his birth, that the elder brother would serve the younger? We are not told, but, assuming he knew of it, he would have reasoned that the promise could not be fulfilled while Esau had all the privileges traditionally conferred on the firstborn, in accordance with the Jewish law of family inheritance. When his older brother came in from the field, starving hungry, Jacob used the opportunity to turn Esau's necessity to his own advantage and tricked him into selling his birthright (vv. 29–34).

Later (Genesis 27), Rebekah colludes further with Jacob to deceive Esau and her husband Isaac. When Isaac becomes blind with old age, realising that he needs to bless his firstborn before he dies, he asks Esau to hunt game and prepare a final meal for him. While Esau is out hunting, Rebekah helps Jacob to disguise himself as Esau by wearing a hairy animal skin. Isaac, assuming the young man before him is Esau, blesses Jacob before Esau returns, only to discover too late that he has blessed the wrong son. Jacob is then forced to flee to his uncle Laban's home, where he is deceived into marrying Laban's older daughter, Leah, instead of the younger, Rachel, whom he preferred (Genesis 29:21–30). Deception continued to play a huge part in the lives of this family, because they were continually trying to pre-empt God's plans rather than allowing his work to unfold in their lives at the appointed times.

Here we are given a glimpse of just how complex life can be, with endless choices between less-than-perfect alternatives. This is also a crucial stage in the development of Abraham's lineage, which, for better or worse, will serve God's purposes in the development of the Israelite nation. Isaac and Rebekah, Jacob and Esau share both good and bad character traits upon which the nation's future leadership will be built. Jacob becomes Israel, whose energy will be directed by the covenant with God, while Esau becomes the founder of a rival nation. (Eventually, the two brothers are reconciled: see Genesis 33).

The struggle between brothers becomes a significant theme throughout the Bible—for example, as in the story of Joseph and his eleven brothers (Genesis 37 to 45) and Jesus' parable of the prodigal son and his elder brother (Luke 15:11–32). In the story of Jacob and Esau, we observe a fascinating insight into the trials of parenting in the midst of sibling rivalry.

Spiritual exercise

❖ What details in the passage strike you the most?
❖ How does this story reveal God's plans working through ordinary, flawed individuals and families?
❖ Reflect on a time of struggle in your own life, either with God or within another relationship. What has this struggle taught you most about yourself?

Prayer

God of relationships,
just as Jacob and Esau struggled in life,
Edom and Israel struggled to survive—
one family, two nations, divided among themselves.
In all my struggles keep me close to you,
my God, my Saviour, and bring me home to you. Amen

Reflection

Jacob and Esau clashed from before birth and each parent favoured one over the other. This Lent, let us reflect on how we can offer unconditional love despite our personal preferences.

Jeremiah and the potter

This is the word that came to Jeremiah from the Lord: 'Go down to the potter's house, and there I will give you my message.' So I went down to the potter's house, and I saw him working at the wheel. But the pot he was shaping from the clay was marred in his hands; so the potter formed it into another pot, shaping it as seemed best to him. Then the word of the Lord came to me: 'O house of Israel, can I not do with you as this potter does?' declares the Lord. 'Like clay in the hand of the potter, so are you in my hand, O house of Israel.'

JEREMIAH 18:1–6

What did Jeremiah see that was so significant in the potter's house? First there was the clay. As he watched the potter shaping and moulding the clay, Jeremiah knew that he was looking at himself, at every person, and at every nation: we are all clay in God's hands. Isaiah (45:9; 64:8) joins with Jeremiah in using the image of the potter and the clay, and in Romans 9:21–22 Paul picks up the same idea. Jeremiah saw that there was often some imperfection in the clay, which spoiled the pot, so the potter broke up the clay and started again, reshaping it into a vessel that pleased him.

Jeremiah saw the potter's wheel turning constantly,

bringing the clay against the potter's hand. Does the wheel represent the changing circumstances of life, under the control of God the potter? If our life is being shaped and moulded by the great Potter, it is our circumstances that bring us again and again under his hand, under the pressure of his moulding fingers, so that he shapes the vessel according to his will. This pressure is finely balanced: too much would crush the vessel and too little would have no impact, but when the precise balance of pressure is applied, the vessel can be made whole and ready to use.

Jeremiah knew that God was the great Potter, with absolute power and control over the clay, to make it what he wanted it to be—to create whatever he chose. How often we resist or try to avoid change! We do not want to be remoulded or reshaped. When we are frightened or weary of adapting, or when our emotional pain and spiritual blindness have locked us into places, patterns or attitudes that require a great deal of loving strength to be overcome, it can feel impossible to allow such change in our lives. Our fear and pain are like flaws in the clay of our lives, flaws that have been part of us for many years and stop us from being all that we could be. They seem an inescapable part of us, yet the Potter can heal and transform us with his hands if we let him, and if we dare to let go.

✣

Spiritual exercise

❖ Imagine you are clay in God's hands. How does it feel to be held by God?

❖ Which parts of you are unyielding and which parts yearn for his gentleness and touch?

❖ Now imagine you are a clay pot. What is your size and shape? Which parts of you are smooth and finished, and which are damaged?

❖ What would you like to be put into this pot? What would you like to be poured out?

Prayer

God of relationships,
you are the potter who works at the wheel
until his pots are finished and whole.
I am your hope-filled vessel.
Open my heart, that your grace may be poured in;
open my hands, that your love can be poured out.
Shape me; bend me; mould me to your glory.
Amen

Reflection

The potter and his clay are dependent on their relationship as Creator and created. This Lent, may we let Christ re-shape us with his sacrificial touch.

Pity and mercy

In reply Jesus said: 'A man was going down from Jerusalem to Jericho, when he fell into the hands of robbers. They stripped him of his clothes, beat him and went away, leaving him half dead. A priest happened to be going down the same road, and when he saw the man, he passed by on the other side. So too, a Levite, when he came to the place and saw him, passed by on the other side. But a Samaritan, as he travelled, came where the man was; and when he saw him, he took pity on him. He went to him and bandaged his wounds, pouring on oil and wine. Then he put the man on his own donkey, took him to an inn and took care of him. The next day he took out two silver coins and gave them to the innkeeper. "Look after him," he said, "and when I return, I will reimburse you for any extra expense you may have." 'Which of these three do you think was a neighbour to the man who fell into the hands of robbers?' The expert in the law replied, 'The one who had mercy on him.' Jesus told him, 'Go and do likewise.'
LUKE 10:30–37

The key themes in this parable are compassion, action and care, and we learn that knowing the right thing is very different from doing it. To understand the context, we need to look first to the conversation that comes before the story, when a lawyer asks Jesus, 'Teacher,

46

what must I do to inherit eternal life?' (v. 25). Luke tells us that the lawyer put the question to Jesus as a test, but he might simply have been seeking understanding of how to interpret the Mosaic Law. Jesus responds by asking the man what he knows the law to say, so the lawyer answers by quoting Deuteronomy 6:5 and Leviticus 19:18: 'Love the Lord your God with all your heart and with all your soul and with all your strength and with all your mind' and 'Love your neighbour as yourself.'

Jesus points out that this kind of love requires more than emotions; it includes practice (v. 28). The lawyer realises that this is very hard: there will always be people whom he cannot love, because he has been brought up to recognise certain people as enemies or those to avoid. Thus he tries to restrict the Law's command by limiting its parameters and asking the question, 'Who is my neighbour?' In response, Jesus tells the parable of the good Samaritan.

The Samaritans were an ethnic group from the northern kingdom of Israel who had intermarried with non-Jews and did not keep all of the Law, so 'true' Jews would have nothing to do with them. This is what made Jesus' conversation with the Samaritan woman at the well so shocking to his disciples (John 4:1–42), and this parable was just as shocking to his Jewish audience. Jesus does not say whether the injured man in the story is a Jew or Gentile, but it makes no difference to the Samaritan, who sees only a person in dire need. He dresses the man's wounds with wine (to disinfect) and oil (to soothe the pain), takes him to an inn to recover and pays the innkeeper with his own money.

The good Samaritan offered compassion, action and care, and Jesus now asks the lawyer if he can follow that example in his own life. Notice that the lawyer cannot bring himself to say the word 'Samaritan' but refers to 'the one who had mercy' (v. 37). Jesus leads the lawyer to answer his own question, demonstrating a most effective way of enabling a person to learn—by guiding them though their own thoughts so that the journey to realisation is their own.

The fact that it was a priest and then a Levite who passed by and ignored the victim is utterly scandalous and a real eye-opener: people who might have been expected to help did not, while someone who would have been despised by the victim (and Jesus' audience) did help. The priest may have had a reasonable excuse not to stop, since touching what might already have been a dead body would have made him unclean according to the Law. He may have decided that being ritually clean was more important than saving someone else's life. It is worth noting, by the way, how scandalous it was that Jesus touched so many 'unclean' people. That was another reason why the Pharisees became so angry with him: he was undermining the very rituals by which they defined their own holiness.

The Samaritan was considered inferior by the Jews, yet he it was who saw the wounded man as his neighbour in need. He moved towards the injured man. This is significant because we must move towards people in order to love them, in order to build a relationship. It doesn't just happen, and nor does it happen at our convenience. The Samaritan moves towards someone who, if he were conscious, would despise him, towards someone who would not do the same if their situations were reversed. This is real vulnerability!

Spiritual exercises

❖ How can you be a good Samaritan in your local church and community?
❖ Reflect on any barriers you find in your own heart to offering a stranger or enemy genuine compassion.
❖ Can we truly love our neighbours as ourselves if we don't love ourselves in the first place? How might we learn to love ourselves?

Prayer

God of relationships,
the lawyer learnt his lesson for life—
the Samaritan moved towards the man in need,
his compassion consuming all prejudice,
while the Levite and priest passed by.
May I show mercy to all people,
and heal the wounds of division. Amen

Reflection

My neighbour is anyone who needs my help, no matter what I feel or know about them. This Lent, may I move towards Christ and, in so doing, reach out to people in need.

This is my body

When evening came, Jesus arrived with the Twelve. While they were reclining at the table eating, he said, 'I tell you the truth, one of you will betray me—one who is eating with me.' They were saddened, and one by one they said to him, 'Surely not I?' 'It is one of the Twelve,' he replied, 'one who dips bread into the bowl with me. The Son of Man will go just as it is written about him. But woe to that man who betrays the Son of Man! It would be better for him if he had not been born.' While they were eating, Jesus took bread, gave thanks and broke it, and gave it to his disciples, saying, 'Take it; this is my body.' Then he took the cup, gave thanks and offered it to them, and they all drank from it. 'This is my blood of the covenant, which is poured out for many,' he said to them. 'I tell you the truth, I will not drink again of the fruit of the vine until that day when I drink it anew in the kingdom of God.'

MARK 14:17–25

This is one of the most moving events in the passion narratives, because it is the last supper, the final meal shared by Jesus and all his disciples before his death, which became the Christian Eucharist or Holy Communion. 'Eucharist' comes from the Greek for 'thanksgiving', as it recalls the thanksgiving prayers from the Jewish Passover tradition, celebrated every year in memory of their deliverance from slavery in Egypt.

One of the Passover festival rituals was the sacrifice of a spotless lamb. In his suffering and death, Jesus himself became the Passover sacrifice, the 'Lamb of God' who takes away the sins of the world (John 1:29). Therefore, the Eucharist is both the source and summit of our Christian life, as it commemorates Christ's surrendering of his own body and blood to the world. In his transformation of the Passover meal, Jesus showed that eating the bread and drinking the wine could now remind us how he has opened the way to the Father, his body broken and his blood poured out.

In our Bible passage, notice first that while the twelve disciples are eating, Jesus breaks the shocking news that one of them will betray him. Mark records that Jesus had spoken twice before of being betrayed to his death (9:31; 10:33), yet the disciples had not totally understood what Jesus had said on those earlier occasions. They clearly did not imagine that any one of them—Jesus' closest friends and followers—would want to betray the man they all loved. Nor did they remotely suspect Judas, which is why each one, in turn, asked Jesus if they were to be his betrayer.

In Jesus' culture, to be betrayed by one 'who is eating with me', who 'dips bread into the bowl with me', was considered especially perfidious. To eat with someone implied friendship, trust and an ongoing obligation to help and protect that person. By speaking of their eating together, and saying that the betrayer is sitting with him as 'one of the Twelve', Jesus is emphasising the enormity of the impending evil. It is also interesting that he echoes Psalm 41:9, in which David prophesies the betrayal, saying, 'Even my close friend, whom I trusted, he who shared my bread, has lifted up his heel against me.'

One of Jesus' earthly missions was to teach his disciples about the future kingdom of God on earth. As Jesus instituted the Eucharist, he took a meal that celebrated Israel's liberation—a past event—and transformed it into a meal that looked forward to a future event, a new kingdom. Therefore, Jesus holds together the past, the present and the future in one real but also symbolic act. In sharing this meal, we all share in his passion and resurrection.

✛

Spiritual exercise

❖ Imagine you are sitting among the disciples with Jesus at the last supper. What do you notice most?
❖ What emotions are present in this Bible passage?
❖ Recall a time when you felt betrayed by someone or several people. Are you able to reflect on that betrayal through different eyes now?

Prayer

God of relationships,
your Son blessed bread and wine around a wooden table
and shared them with his disciples;
one of them would betray Jesus, though they knew it not.
Just as the sun rises, so Christ will rise;
just as wine is poured, so Christ will pour out his life
and renew his kingdom here on earth.
Amen

Reflection

Jesus showed us perfect love by his sacrifice in the face of betrayal. This Lent, let us be confident in our faith and not betray him in thoughts, words or deeds.

Put on love

Therefore, as God's chosen people, holy and dearly loved, clothe yourselves with compassion, kindness, humility, gentleness and patience. Bear with each other and forgive whatever grievances you may have against one another. Forgive as the Lord forgave you. And over all these virtues put on love, which binds them all together in perfect unity. Let the peace of Christ rule in your hearts, since as members of one body you were called to peace. And be thankful. Let the word of Christ dwell in you richly as you teach and admonish one another with all wisdom, and as you sing psalms, hymns and spiritual songs with gratitude in your hearts to God. And whatever you do, whether in word or deed, do it all in the name of the Lord Jesus, giving thanks to God the Father through him.

COLOSSIANS 3:12–17

Colosse was a city in what is now south-west Turkey. It had a thriving wool and textile industry and a significant Jewish population, although most Christians there were Gentile and there were many pagan influences challenging their faith. In his letter to the Colossian Christians, Paul was trying to encourage them in their belief and to help them avoid syncretism—that is, the reconciling and practising of different religions and philosophies on an equal footing with each other.

The passage we read here comes immediately after Paul's outline of what is basic Christian behaviour, in which he instructs the Colossians about what they should not do and explains why those particular acts do not lead to God. However, in this passage his instructions are positive, and are concerned with what we should do in order to deepen our relationship with God and our fellow believers. The context of Paul's thinking is that as we have died with Christ, we therefore need to put on a new self according to the image that God has chosen for us. This means that the old 'me' has been discarded because I am born again in Christ. If I have accepted Christ into my heart, I need to think and act in ways that show that this acceptance is real. Paul then describes the virtues with which we should now clothe ourselves.

The Greek verb for 'to put on' is *enduo*, which means 'to sink or slip into (clothing); to clothe oneself'. It occurs in Colossians 3 in verse 10 and then again in verse 14. In the Old Testament, there are many images and symbols of being clothed in the presence of God, or being clothed in power, protected or shielded (for example, Exodus 23:20 and Psalm 91:4), so the use of this image is entirely in keeping with Paul's desire to draw on the rich heritage of the scriptures. By alluding to other biblical texts, he would have urged his audience to understand both the physical and spiritual nuances of what he is saying.

The list of virtues given by Paul is not exhaustive but we notice that it represents many of the qualities that are important in the way we handle all our relationships. We learn that love is the most important of all the virtues mentioned, because it is the fulfilment of every other act or expression. We are called to love because God first loved us. The use of the word 'bind' in verse 14 is especially evocative because, when we are bound by something, we can feel either burdened by it or liberated by its promise. To be bound to God through love provides us with a sense of security and stability. While, in the Old Testament, the call to love our God and each other is very strong, Paul continues to show how Jesus fulfils both the Ten Commandments and the rest of the Law by taking this love one stage further. Here, love is rooted firmly within our hearts but is also something that we need to wear on the outside; thus the body and the soul are united in the expression of love.

We all know that forgiveness comes more easily from a heart transformed through compassion, kindness, humility, gentleness and patience. Yet being forgiven can be much harder! When forgiveness is genuinely offered and received, unity is restored, and this unity can be sustained only where there is sincere love. Unity, in this passage from Colossians, means the way we order our relationships through Christ. Such unity was very important in Paul's time, when competing ideologies distracted early believers from their focus on Christ. To show unity demonstrated to unbelievers that the Church of Jesus could and did work in practice, that it enabled harmonious living and mirrored a coherent and consistent expression of early Christian truths.

✥

Spiritual exercise

❖ Reflect on the virtues that we are invited to mirror in this passage. Which virtues are attractive to you? Which virtues are hard to imitate?

❖ Which of your spiritual clothes need mending and which don't fit any more?

Prayer

God of relationships,
you chose me from the beginning
to become who I truly am.
As I clothe myself in your name,
help me to put on love each day.
May peace be woven into the fabric of my soul
and compassion threaded through all my deeds. Amen

Reflection

We must become what we are called to be through Christ.
During Lent, what must I do to clothe myself in Christ?

✛

Forgiveness

The weak can never forgive. Forgiveness is the attribute of the strong.

MAHATMA GANDHI (1869–1948)

In the Bible, forgiveness is an important concept which develops from being an act of duty to being an act of charity. This development reaches its climax in the New Testament, when Jesus commands his followers to forgive each other numerous times (Matthew 18:22). He also includes forgiveness in the Lord's Prayer in Matthew 6:9–15 and Luke 11:2–4, which says, 'Forgive us our debts/sins, as we also have forgiven our debtors/everyone who sins against us.' We find numerous examples of genuine forgiveness in the Bible, including the stories of Esau and Jacob (Genesis 33:4–15), Joseph (45:8–15), Moses (Numbers 12:1–13), David (2 Samuel 19:18–23), Solomon (1 Kings 1:52–53), Jesus (Luke 23:34), Stephen (Acts 7:59–60) and Paul (2 Timothy 4:16).

Forgiveness is one of the hardest things to bestow or (as suggested previously) to receive in life. How often do we forgive ourselves or truly believe that God has forgiven us? Sometimes it is much easier to indulge our shame and guilt than it is to accept God's renewal of of situation. We know we would rather be at peace, but why should *we* be the initiator of reconciliation? Why should *we* be proactive? All the while, when we are investing energy in managing our wounds and hurts, our vision is narrowed. Our emotional baggage not only gives us a heavy heart but also filters into other areas of our lives. It has the potential to hurt and damage the people around us who are innocent as far as our suffering is concerned. So we could ask ourselves, how much more energy are we willing to invest in this hurt?

If we acknowledge that we would rather be free of a destructive wound, then we have taken the first steps to accepting that we have a choice as to whether to stay still or to consider a way forward. Forgiveness is an act of the imagination as well as the heart. If we can imagine being free again, of not holding on to the situation, we are more likely to be able to work out how it might happen. Of course, we all know that even if we take the right steps to reconcile ourselves with the person, people or situation that hurts us, others may either fail to recognise the hurt inflicted or reject our approaches. We may also resist other people's attempts to say sorry, no matter who is in the wrong.

However, if we do not try at all, we still have to face ourselves. This is why praying for humility and grace to forgive, asking for the courage and wisdom to make the first step, is such a significant process. Even if the people we need to forgive are no longer in contact with us, or have died, we can still offer forgiveness and ask for healing between this world and the next. The turning point is when we have changed inside and are no longer prisoners to our pain or bound by our pride. In that moment, we have truly let go and let God in.

We live our lives forwards but understand them backwards, and, with forgiveness, we have a choice as to how we wish our future to be shaped. This choice is the fulcrum on which hangs the future peace in our lives, and it is an important concept in the Bible. The Greek word *metanoia* means 'repentance'—a fundamental change in character or way of life, or spiritual conversion. It is a compound word, combining the word for 'after' with the word for 'thinking'. The first part of the word denotes a change over time, so the whole meaning is 'to think differently afterwards'. *Metanoia*, then, is an afterthought in which a change of mind enables a change of conduct or, as is commonly said, a change of heart and mind. In Hebrew, the idea of repentance has a different nuance. It is represented by two verbs meaning 'to return' and 'to feel sorrow', and thus evokes a sense of empathy as well as a change of behaviour. A good example of these nuances is demonstrated in the story of the prodigal son, which we shall read later in this section.

The theologian Paul Tillich, in his book *The Eternal Now* (SCM, 2002), said that 'forgiveness is the highest form of forgetting because it is forgetting in spite of remembering' (ch. 2). We are not asked to pretend that our wounds never existed but to acknowledge that they do not need to remain wounds for ever. Jesus shows us that there is always another way of looking at the same problem and of handling this complex dynamic. His dying on the cross was the ultimate act of forgiveness

I am your brother

Then Joseph could no longer control himself before all his attendants, and he cried out, 'Have everyone leave my presence!' So there was no one with Joseph when he made himself known to his brothers. And he wept so loudly that the Egyptians heard him, and Pharaoh's household heard about it. Joseph said to his brothers, 'I am Joseph! Is my father still living?' But his brothers were not able to answer him, because they were terrified at his presence. Then Joseph said to his brothers, 'Come close to me.' When they had done so, he said, 'I am your brother Joseph, the one you sold into Egypt! And now, do not be distressed and do not be angry with yourselves for selling me here, because it was to save lives that God sent me ahead of you...' Then he threw his arms around his brother Benjamin and wept, and Benjamin embraced him, weeping. And he kissed all his brothers and wept over them. Afterward his brothers talked with him.

GENESIS 45:1–5, 14–15

This passage is one of the most powerful Old Testament examples of forgiveness. It shows both the grieving process at the loss of family relationships over many years and the painful journey to reconciliation and peace. First we see Joseph needing space and privacy to weep again, as he had done previously when his brothers, not recognising him, confessed their original sin against him (Genesis 42:21–24). This time, however, the momentum is carried forward in a different way. Joseph's brothers appear dumbstruck because they are shocked to see their brother both alive and standing in front of them, and because they fear punishment, having sold him into slavery more than 20 years before. The Hebrew word for 'terrified' here includes the sentiments of being amazed or frightened.

We see that Joseph does not diminish what his brothers did to him, but he also sees that God's purpose is greater than his brothers' past wrongdoing. It is with this insight that he is able to kiss his brothers and weep over them. Neither is he selective: his compassion is showed consistently to all his siblings. His are tears of tenderness, rooted in strong affection, despite everything he suffered because of his brothers' cruelty long ago.

Instead of showing rightly deserved anger or delight in the famine's implications for his brothers, Joseph takes their crime upon himself: 'God sent me ahead of you...' The family of Israel, of Jacob, is the particular focus of God's providence. Joseph believed that his promotion was designed not so much to save the Egyptian nation as to preserve his own small family. Even though his brothers had plotted to defeat his dreams by selling him into Egypt, God had planned to fulfil them.

Genesis 45 also tells how Joseph promises to take care of his father and family during the remaining years of famine (see v. 11). He urges that his father should be informed of his new life and status immediately. His brothers must rush back to Canaan and tell Jacob that his son Joseph is not only alive but is now lord over Egypt.

The climax of this story is not just about forgiveness but about unity. There is a fascinating theory on the coloured coat that Joseph had worn as a sign of his father's favour (see 37:3–4). Some scholars argue that the Hebrew words for this coat make up a compound phrase using all the names of the twelve tribes of Israel (the twelve sons of Jacob). Thus, when Joseph initially wears the coat, the tribes are united but, when his brothers rip off his coat and sell him into slavery, the tribes are broken apart. Now that Joseph makes peace with his brothers, we see tribal unity restored, and Israel made whole.

Spiritual exercise

❖ What strikes you most about the different emotions and dynamics in this passage?

❖ Are there people in your own circles of family or friends whom you have not seen in years? How would you feel if you saw them again?

❖ What does Joseph teach you most about forgiveness here?

Prayer

Forgiving Father,
Joseph wept loudly for his brothers;
he wept for time lost and time regained.
After his grief and revelations
he forgave those who had rejected him.
Lord, show me the way to forgive those who hurt me
and restore unity in my life and theirs.
Amen

Reflection

Forgiveness is a gift that must begin with me, even if I have done no wrong. This Lent, may I reach out with courage and grace to those I need to forgive, including myself.

not want to listen and learn, the people still to come might do so. It is both a historic and a prophetic psalm.

In the opening verses, the psalmist describes God's infinite compassion for the Israelites as he delivered them out of Egyptian captivity, bringing them through the harsh desert and into his promised land. All the time, the Israelites complained, seeming to overlook the extraordinary miracles God performed to sustain them on the way. On the one hand, they knew that God was their redeemer but, on the other, they abused God's generosity with their manipulative demands.

In this passage from the psalm, the Israelites are first accused of perfidiousness. They show neither repentance nor sorrow for their infidelity towards the God who, they simultaneously acknowledge, has rescued them. Their heads and hearts act separately, because they do not realise that serving God requires loyalty from the heart first and the lips second. It does not occur to them that God knows that their outward manifestations of love and praise are shallow and meaningless. Their relentless disobedience and provocation of God in the desert neither enhance their relationship with him nor build them up as a nation. How does God handle this constant treachery?

We read that God's response is one of enormous patience. He offers mercy and repeated forgiveness, despite the stubborn and ignorant attitudes of the people. He holds back his anger and his hand, at least for now; he remembers that they are mortal. The very fact that humans are flesh and blood means that their bodies are transient: the psalmist compares them with a puff of wind, a passing breeze (v. 39). The fragility of humanity is what inspires God to be compassionate and loving towards those he has made.

Spiritual exercise

- ❖ Reflect on the nature of religious hypocrisy. Do you see hypocrisy in your church and society today?
- ❖ Why do you think the Israelites found it so hard to obey God?
- ❖ Which aspects of your relationship with God are highlighted by this psalm?

Prayer

Forgiving Father,
throughout history we have failed you.
We have tried and tested your love,
misused your kindness and power.
Help me to repent of my sins
and, with a sincere heart,
come to you once more for mercy. Amen

Reflection

At all times and in all ages, God is both patient and compassionate with individuals and nations, because he believes that we need his infinite love. How best can you show God your genuine loyalty this Lent?

A long way off

But while he was still a long way off, his father saw him and was filled with compassion for him; he ran to his son, threw his arms around him and kissed him. The son said to him, 'Father, I have sinned against heaven and against you. I am no longer worthy to be called your son.' But the father said to his servants, 'Quick! Bring the best robe and put it on him. Put a ring on his finger and sandals on his feet. Bring the fattened calf and kill it. Let's have a feast and celebrate. For this son of mine was dead and is alive again; he was lost and is found.' So they began to celebrate.

Meanwhile, the older son was in the field. When he came near the house, he heard music and dancing. So he called one of the servants and asked him what was going on. 'Your brother has come,' he replied, 'and your father has killed the fattened calf because he has him back safe and sound.' The older brother became angry and refused to go in. So his father went out and pleaded with him. But he answered his father, 'Look! All these years I've been slaving for you and never disobeyed your orders. Yet you never gave me even a young goat so I could celebrate with my friends. But when this son of yours who has squandered your property with prostitutes comes home, you kill the fattened calf for him!' 'My son,' the father said, 'you are always with me, and everything I have is yours.'

LUKE 15:20–31

The focus of this parable is usually on the wayward son who journeys into a far country, then comes to his senses and returns home, or the older brother who is consumed by anger, resentment and self-righteousness and refuses to show generosity. Why does he have such strong feelings? Perhaps it is because his goodness has not been given sufficient recognition by the father. He would really prefer the father to punish his younger brother rather than welcome him home so easily. He wants to be told how right and good he has been—and, of course, in one sense he has been more loyal.

In fact, we can see ourselves in each of these characters, perhaps in the weakness of the younger son, the bitterness of the older brother, or the compassion of the father—God, the one who embraces us all and offers us a chance to start again.

This Bible story is usually read as indicating the following sequence: repentance, confession, forgiveness. The assumption is that forgiveness requires repentance first. Yet there is another reading of the story in which the central act is the running of the father to greet the returning sinner. His son has broken the strict code of the community of which he was a part. His request to receive his inheritance before it is rightfully his is an insult to his father and should have led to punishment for arrogant rebellion. Instead, the broken-hearted father gives him what should legally have been passed down only after his own death. The son promptly wastes his precious inheritance and even becomes ritually impure by living among pigs. He decides to return home, hoping for a job—but is he truly repentant or is he simply trying his luck again?

In returning, however, he places himself in great danger, because he must run the gauntlet of the village elders, guardians of the community's moral code, before he can get to his father and make his plea for work. If the elders see him enter the village, they will break an earthenware vessel over his head as a sign that he has shattered his covenant with the community and he may be offered nothing because he is already dead to them. The sorrowful father knows this and has therefore been watching out for him, which is why he sees him before anyone else does. Then he runs to meet him. Running was also an extraordinary break of the patriarchal code, which specified that the greater your dignity, the more slowly you moved.

The waiting father, however, has no interest in his own dignity or status. He rushes out to meet and embrace his disgraced child. It is this abandonment of the correct moral code and the principle that forgiveness is conditional on repentance that forms the scandalous heart of the story. The son is clearly forgiven by the father before he can get a word out, and when he does produce his prepared speech there is a significant omission: there is no plea for a job on the farm (compare verse 21 with verse 19). This reading of the parable suggests that the father's outpouring of love causes a true change of heart in his son, so the forgiveness freely given calls forth the repentance that follows it.

The parable ends inconclusively, however, with an act of petulant defiance of the father by the elder brother.

Here, again, the father ignores the traditional code by explaining the nature of his rejoicing at the return of his younger son. Since the parable stops at this point, we do not know whether the older son also responds to the unconditional love of the father with his own change of heart. We do know, though, that this father is not one who establishes categories of reward and punishment, or who sees his sons as rivals for his affection and his property. He loves them equally.

Both sons have a basic choice to make: will they see themselves in terms of the father's love or not? There is a similar choice before us, as we consider the unconditional forgiveness held out to us by God.

Spiritual exercise

❖ Recall a time when you did not feel worthy of another person's kindness. What emotion does this memory evoke in you now?

❖ Do you have any emotional wounds that you know need healing? What might you do to begin the process of forgiving and healing yourself and the other person or people concerned?

Prayer

Forgiving Father,
when I squander my soul
on life's passing distractions,
may I not lose sight of your love.
May I not abuse your patient waiting
while I come to my senses
and run home to you once more.
Amen

Reflection

We cannot forgive if that which binds us cannot be loosened.
This Lent, ask God to show you how to loosen the ties of
hurt, pain and pride.

The one I kiss

Just as he was speaking, Judas, one of the Twelve,
appeared. With him was a crowd armed with swords and
clubs, sent from the chief priests, the teachers of the law,
and the elders. Now the betrayer had arranged a signal
with them: 'The one I kiss is the man; arrest him and lead
him away under guard.' Going at once to Jesus, Judas
said, 'Rabbi!' and kissed him. The men seized Jesus and
arrested him. Then one of those standing near drew his
sword and struck the servant of the high priest, cutting
off his ear. 'Am I leading a rebellion,' said Jesus, 'that you
have come out with swords and clubs to capture me?
Every day I was with you, teaching in the temple courts,
and you did not arrest me. But the Scriptures must be
fulfilled.' Then everyone deserted him and fled.

MARK 14:43–50

In our fourth reading on relationships, in the passage
from Mark 14 where Jesus shared the last supper with
his disciples, he predicted that one of them would
betray him. Now, in this passage, we come to the
moment when Judas carries out the deed. Here we see
Jesus' foreknowledge of the betrayal—as the fulfilment
of the scriptures—and the desertion by his followers.
Mark's Gospel states that the chief priests had been
looking for a devious way to arrest Jesus (14:1). They

did not want to arrest him during the Passover feast as they knew that the people would probably riot, and this frightened them enormously. Instead, they chose the night before the feast: at night their actions would be cloaked by darkness.

For the word translated 'kiss', both Mark and Matthew (26:48–49) use the Greek verb *kataphilein*, which means 'to kiss firmly, intensely or tenderly'. Such a kiss was the traditional greeting given to a teacher, and this underlines the gravity of the betrayal further: it was no light-hearted or accidental embrace. What we have here is a combination of deception and desertion, compounded by an act of violation: to give a show of intimacy while also distancing oneself from a person is surely a contradiction.

Judas' betrayal of Jesus is made more puzzling by the fact that we are not told why he wanted to betray his master. Was his role merely a functional device, intended simply to fulfil the prophecies? Would Jesus have been able to prevent the betrayal, or was it necessary for our future salvation? If Judas were merely the negotiator in a pre-agreed deal, what does that say about both Judas' earlier relationship with Jesus and his ultimate destiny? Was Judas capable of discernment or not? Was he able to make a conscious choice to betray or save Jesus? What do Christians today need to learn most from this most difficult of episodes in the passion narratives?

Judas has become synonymous with betrayal just as Thomas has become synonymous with doubt; they are convenient scapegoats for believers and, as such, are often used to make a wider point about the difference between good and evil. Yet Jesus gave Thomas another chance to believe, but he simply acknowledges the fact that Judas will betray him. Judas' character proves that only God knows what lies in the human heart and only God can resolve the most mysterious of actions. If, in today's reading, we are presented with ultimate betrayal, we are also challenged to surrender our judgments upon other human beings and leave them at the feet of Christ.

Spiritual exercise

- ❖ Imagine how Jesus felt, knowing that Judas would betray him imminently.
- ❖ Imagine how Jesus felt, knowing that everyone had deserted him at this crucial moment of his life.
- ❖ Have you ever felt betrayed or abandoned by those you love? Can you forgive them now?

Prayer

Forgiving Father,
Judas betrayed your Son with a kiss,
but we are just as guilty now—
we do not always defend you
in the face of those who defy you.
Yet you died for us while we were ignorant and sinful:
our infidelity will never match your grace. Amen

What is truth?

Pilate then went back inside the palace, summoned Jesus and asked him, 'Are you the king of the Jews?' 'Is that your own idea,' Jesus asked, 'or did others talk to you about me?' 'Am I a Jew?' Pilate replied. 'It was your people and your chief priests who handed you over to me. What is it you have done?' Jesus said, 'My kingdom is not of this world. If it were, my servants would fight to prevent my arrest by the Jews. But now my kingdom is from another place.' 'You are a king, then!' said Pilate. Jesus answered, 'You are right in saying I am a king. In fact, for this reason I was born, and for this I came into the world, to testify to the truth. Everyone on the side of truth listens to me.' 'What is truth?' Pilate asked. With this he went out again to the Jews and said, 'I find no basis for a charge against him. But it is your custom for me to release to you one prisoner at the time of the Passover. Do you want me to release "the king of the Jews"?' They shouted back, 'No, not him! Give us Barabbas!'

JOHN 18:33–40

Despite being a powerful man, in a position of great authority bestowed by an empire that had conquered the known world, Pilate was human. He had exactly the same fears that most people have regarding their popularity and capability—but those in power have a longer way to fall when they fail. Pilate was naturally apprehensive that his job was on the line if he lost control of the situation. Meeting Jesus altered his life for ever. This conversation, recorded in John's Gospel (also Matthew 27:11–14; Mark 15:1–5; Luke 23:1–5), forced him to choose between his fears for himself and an understanding of the truth. While Pilate wrestled with his conscience, the Son of God stood serenely watching and, with grace, allowed his destiny to unfold.

Pilate had something that the Jewish religious leaders really wanted: supreme political authority. In a flash, he could make decisions that the people under him would obey immediately, and this was important to those who wanted to get rid of Jesus yet did not have the power to kill him themselves. They therefore decided to accuse Jesus before Pilate with two lies—that Jesus was teaching others to stop paying taxes to Rome and that he was inciting a popular rebellion to counter Rome's authority by declaring himself as king (see Luke 23:2).

If these accusations were true, then Pilate would feel that he was betraying Rome by refusing to address Jesus' crimes. The religious leaders had malevolently counterposed Jesus against Rome, even though Jesus always respected Roman civil authority and had previously shown no disobedience to Roman law. Pilate understood, however, that the main issue was that Jesus threatened the religious leaders' own power and position among the people. What they were really objecting to was Jesus' authority over them rather than his relationship with Pilate.

As Jesus calmly moves closer to his death through

this religious and political turmoil, he takes command of the conversation with Pilate. He draws Pilate ineluctably to question the real issues that are before them both in this discussion. Thus Pilate is forced to confront his own commitment to truth. When he asks, 'What is truth?' he is not really very concerned about absolute truth or its purpose in this context: what he wants is rescue from this situation. Jesus was a Galilean, which technically meant that he came from Herod's territory, so Pilate tried dispatching Jesus to Herod (Luke 23:6–12), thinking he could avoid the responsibility once and for all. In addition, Pilate's wife had been troubled by a dream about the innocence of Jesus (Matthew 27:19), and she shared this with her husband. It was as if God was giving Pilate different signs to convey the prisoner's innocence, and all Pilate needed to do was to face the extraordinary truth about Jesus.

Yet the chief priests, elders and lawyers—in fact, the entire Sanhedrin and the wicked and foolish mob— were not going to accept one simple 'no' for an answer, even if it was from the governor of Judea. By protesting against Jesus' innocence, they implied that Pilate was not doing his job properly, and that could only mean one thing: he was committing treason. By this stage, Pilate was cornered by a crowd of manipulators, clearly unable to defend either Jesus or himself.

Not wanting to upset the crowds, Pilate offers amnesty to a prisoner of the people's choice. They choose Barabbas, known to be a 'robber' (John 18:40, RSV). The Greek word for 'robber' had a second meaning in that political context—'resistance fighter'. Barabbas had been part of an uprising and was suspected of murdering someone. Prominent Jewish resistance fighters were perceived as potential messiahs, so in Jesus and Barabbas we have two messianic figures. The difference between them was that people understood Barabbas' crime and the freedom for which he was fighting, but Jesus' 'crime' was both to present a mysterious kingdom in which it was necessary to lose your life in order to save it (John 12:25), and to place himself above the prevailing social order, threatening to change the very structures by which the people lived. The fact that the character of the true Messiah had long been recorded in the Jewish scriptures was tragically overlooked. Thus Pilate, unable to defend truth without damaging his own highly fragile reputation, abandons Jesus, the Son of God, to an unlawful death. Nowhere in the history of all time has pure innocence been so utterly wronged as in this conviction by plain cowardice.

Spiritual exercise

❖ Reflect on the nature of truth and what it means for your own faith.
❖ What does this passage tell you about kingship and power?
❖ What do you learn about crowd pressure?

❖ What could have prevented Pilate from endorsing Jesus' death?

Prayer

Forgiving Father,
in Pilate's hands Jesus is condemned
and swiftly sentenced to death.
Curb me when I am quick to condemn others
through fear, weakness and pride.
Lord, may your truths dwell in my heart
so that I always act in your name only.
Amen

Reflection

Sometimes the truth is painful to admit, especially when it reveals our own failings to the world. This Lent, may we search for the truth and find courage to accept its implications, no matter how humbling it might be for us.

Sacrifice

God cannot suffer, but he can 'suffer with'.

ST BERNARD OF CLAIRVAUX (1090–1153), FROM *COMMENTARY ON THE SONG OF SONGS* (SERMON 26, NO 5).

In the last section, we explored the concept of forgiveness. From the Bible we understand that forgiveness is connected with sacrifice. Sacrifice was very common in the Ancient Near East as a means of religious expression, and took a variety of forms. Gods and goddesses had to be honoured, appeased and thanked regularly, whether for agricultural or human fertility, health, prosperity or deliverance from enemies. Similarly, the primary way of receiving forgiveness in the Old Testament was through the sacrificial system, which formed part of the covenantal relationship between God and Israel. The system involved identifying what was sinful and in need of forgiveness; bringing a sacrifice or sacrifices to offer reparation and show the need for God's help; laying hands on the sacrifice(s) to symbolise identification with the sacrifice(s) made; and finally, if the sacrifice was an animal, killing it in order to release the animal's life blood and wipe out the sin.

This organised system of sacrifice does not manifest itself fully in the Old Testament story until after the exodus. The first seven chapters of Leviticus provide us with the most detailed account of Israel's sacrificial life, using five categories—burnt, grain, peace, sin and guilt offerings. A huge significance was attached to the sacrifice of unblemished animals because they represented the holiness of God. God's pure mercy in renewing his relationship with the sinner was in stark contrast to the blemished nature of the person or people concerned.

The full expression of God's expectations, in terms of the people's response to his forgiveness, appears with the later prophets, who guided the Israelites to a new way of understanding their relationship with God and each other. Micah, Amos, Isaiah, Jeremiah, Ezekiel and Malachi were dynamic opponents of the misuse of sacrifice, especially when it mocked the very God for which it was intended. The mere act of sacrifice was not enough to ensure forgiveness and peace: a change of heart, as well as a real belief in and love of God, were much more important than the mundane mechanics of offering objects, food and animals. The later prophets' emphasis on a repentant heart and interior change was meant to counter the increasing repetitive abuses of the sacrificial system and to prepare the way for the greater sacrifice of Christ in the New Testament.

It should have been no surprise to the Pharisees, therefore, that one of Jesus' recurring themes was that of forgiveness and renewed relationships rather than blind obedience to rules and sacrifices. However, they spectacularly failed to grasp the prophetic warnings of earlier centuries or to understand why Jesus would radically change the priorities within people's personal relationships. He angered the temple dealers who confused business with devotion to God (John 2:13–16), he astonished the teacher of the law with his parable of the good Samaritan story (Luke 10:25–37) and surprised the Samaritan woman at the well (John 4:1–42) with his knowledge of her situation. His friendships with tax collectors, prostitutes and children drove many people to despair, turning their whole behavioural map upside down.

Yet Mary, while following the law by bringing Jesus to the temple and offering a sacrifice of two turtledoves for her own purification (Luke 2:22–24), was humbly eager to do God's will, despite the consequences for her own life, including even the ultimate and perfect sacrifice of her son.

Amos sought to reform the Israelite places of worship by castigating the people who abused them. He is seen by most theologians as a social reformer and a political radical, reminding people of the social implications of their ancient religious traditions. He is therefore highly contemporary in his vision of the sorry state of the world. Amos, like most of the biblical prophets, was unafraid of the powerful rulers of his society— the kings, religious leaders and lawyers. He focused on the oppressed and the poor, and their plight was his motivation for change and challenge. However, his message was unwelcome in Israel. Not only was he a foreigner from the southern kingdom, but his blatant prophecies of doom felt completely at odds with Israel's political climate of hope and prosperity.

At the heart of Amos' message lies a fundamental plea for social justice: 'But let justice roll on like a river, righteousness like a never-failing stream!' (v. 24). Amos was not going to stop until he had made genuine progress. The Israelites were remarkably stubborn but he would make them hear! They had forgotten the most basic demand of their law—respect for their neighbours, whether at home, at the temple or in the marketplace. Amos repeatedly referred to ways in which the people had failed to keep the law and the terms of the covenant described in Exodus 20:22—23:33. He reminded them that they frequently abused the poor for the sake of their own greed, took extensive advantage of debtors, perverted the course of justice and dealt deceitfully, even on the sabbath.

In addition to highlighting their specific legal

offences, Amos pointed out that the Israelites had lost their ability to discern right from wrong. Their worst crime, though, was that their sins had religious roots. The Israelites seriously believed that they could appease God with numerous sacrifices and offerings, failing to see any relationship between worship and basic human justice. Amos was mad with anger at these people's hypocrisy and predicted their inevitable destruction. He decided that the only way to make them see sense was to use shock tactics. What else would shake them out of their selfishness and complacency?

Amos claimed that, time and again, the Israelites had been unfaithful to God. Because of their infidelity, they had no right to worship God and expect blessings in return. The prerequisites of a relationship with God should have been well known to the Israelites by this time, so it was somewhat bizarre that they failed to grasp this simple message—that God desires justice and righteousness above all.

Amos used simple, straightforward language and imagery to communicate the messages he had received from God, hoping that this would encourage Israel, Judah and the neighbouring nations to listen to his warnings. However, he also employed many agricultural metaphors, drawn mostly from his own farming experience, to define what he saw as the inherent corruption of his people. His overall prophetic voice is clear and direct. After his lively condemnations, he concludes his message with a proclamation of hope and restoration for the people of Israel—but only if they mend their ways (Amos 9:9–12). It is their choice.

Spiritual exercise

❖ Reflect on Amos' language and imagery when condemning the Israelites' worship. Are there parallels in the church today?
❖ Who do you think are modern-day prophets?
❖ How do you understand the need for justice in your own faith and in your relationships with others?

Prayer

Giving God,
you gave us the law and we changed its rules;
you taught us to worship and we offered you idols.
You sent your prophet Amos,
who found ancient Israel wanting.
Justice and mercy are what you desire—
so may we empty our hearts of all that is impure
and fill them with righteousness for ever more.
Amen

Reflection

Sometimes we see with too narrow a gaze and fail to comprehend the injustice around us. This Lent, may we renew our vision and take action where there is suffering.

We are healed

Who has believed our message and to whom has the arm of the Lord been revealed? He grew up before him like a tender shoot, and like a root out of dry ground. He had no beauty or majesty to attract us to him, nothing in his appearance that we should desire him. He was despised and rejected by men, a man of sorrows, and familiar with suffering. Like one from whom men hide their faces he was despised, and we esteemed him not. Surely he took up our infirmities and carried our sorrows, yet we considered him stricken by God, smitten by him, and afflicted. But he was pierced for our transgressions, he was crushed for our iniquities; the punishment that brought us peace was upon him, and by his wounds we are healed.

ISAIAH 53:1–5

The prophet Isaiah had already prophesied total destruction for a sinful Judah and for all the other nations that defied God, but the last 27 chapters of the book that bears his name prophesy restoration beyond hope. In the last of the four 'Songs of the suffering servant' is this poetic description of the 'man of sorrows', which later became a common theme in medieval and Christian art. Many Christians interpret these verses as a prophecy of Jesus' coming, having been written roughly 700 years before his birth.

The language of this passage is similar to many of the psalms of lament (such as Psalms 12, 74, 80, 94 and 129) or parts of the book of Job, where prayers of pain and grief are expressed to God, in the expectation of answers, relief, hope or forgiveness. A common theme in laments is rejection by the community. Thus, this text is not a literal description of the servant's or nation's life but a figurative picture describing feelings of total alienation, loneliness, suffering and sorrow. The rejection here is significant because, throughout the Old Testament, the Israelites were convinced that God had chosen them for a special purpose, delivered them from their enemies and promised them an eternal covenant. So why is such categorical rejection described?

When God's people were taken into exile from their land, part of the problem was the way their neighbouring nations perceived the situation. If the Israelites had consistently disobeyed their God and, therefore, God was seen to abandon his people to their enemies, who else would stand witness to this God? The Egyptians, Assyrians and Babylonians all despised the people of Israel, not simply because the Israelites were a political nuisance, but because they did not understand the Israelite religion. If the nation remained in exile, they also remained a nation scorned. A major part of this section of the book of Isaiah (as well as the book of Ezekiel) is devoted to the hope of restoration— yet, until the people showed renewed obedience and fidelity towards God, the timing of this restoration was difficult to predict.

The initial imagery in our passage refers to 'the arm of the Lord'. This is not a military reference so much as a picture of God's will and his use of power. It is followed quickly by the image of a sapling springing up in hostile conditions and therefore never being able to flourish or reach its potential. For Christians, this could be reminiscent of Jesus' roots. He was born in a rough stable in Bethlehem and settled in Nazareth, a place of no great distinction, where he learnt the basic trade of carpentry. In adult life, when Jesus tried to teach in his home synagogue, the leaders were astonished that he preached with such authority. They had seen him grow up and knew his family and could not believe that Jesus was 'claiming' such wisdom. Jesus said, 'Only in his home town… is a prophet without honour' and refused to do many miraculous works there because of the people's unbelief (Matthew 13:57–58). Nathanael's question to Philip, 'Can anything good come from Nazareth?' (John 1:46), is entirely in keeping with the national opinion of Nazareth as an undistinguished place.

Next (v. 2), Isaiah tells us that the figure being described has no beauty or desirable features—in fact, quite the opposite, as he is someone to hide from and avoid. If the suffering servant here is representative of the Messiah, the detail about the person's face is paradoxical. God was considered too holy to see face-to-face, so both Moses and Elijah hid from him, and yet here it is out of derision and not a sense of his holiness that people refuse to look at the Christ-figure.

We move now towards the heartrending account

Prayer

Giving God,
you suffered our sins in silence;
you carried our crimes on a cross.
Outstretched, outcast,
outlived but not outdone.
Your glory is still to come
on the day we sin no more.
Amen

Reflection

Jesus holds all our problems in outstretched arms of love. This Lent, may we renew our understanding of his suffering and complain less about the smaller crosses we have to bear.

All she had

As he looked up, Jesus saw the rich putting their gifts into the temple treasury. He also saw a poor widow put in two very small copper coins. 'I tell you the truth,' he said, 'this poor widow has put in more than all the others. All these people gave their gifts out of their wealth; but she out of her poverty put in all she had to live on.'

LUKE 21:1–4

Jesus sat down opposite the place where financial offerings were placed in the temple. It was located in the Court of the Women, where little boxes were set out to receive worshippers' contributions. Jesus began to watch the crowds going up to present their gifts, but he was impressed not by the amount each person gave, but by how sacrificial their gifts were. He noticed many rich people throwing in large amounts of money very publicly but this failed to gain his respect.

The lesson of the widow's 'mites' or small coins, as described here in Luke and in Mark (12:41–44), is an enduring and profound testament to the value of faith. A destitute widow had almost nothing to give, yet what she had, she gave selflessly as her personal donation to the temple. The coins she gave were pretty much worthless in themselves but it was Jewish custom at that time not to put in fewer than two gifts. Therefore, the widow gave the smallest legal gift possible.

Jesus points out, however, that her small gift was actually worth more than the ostentatious contributions of the wealthy worshippers, since her coins represented all that she had. This holy woman had demonstrated true faith in God with this seemingly insignificant act. She could not know where her next meal would come from, as she did not have the money to plan in advance, but she believed that God would provide for her. In that sacrifice, she showed complete trust.

When Jesus considers the nature of giving here, he thinks of three aspects: motive, attitude and financial status. Why is it important to give, and with what motives were these worshippers contributing? Jesus is warning us that giving for the wrong reasons is not genuine giving: if we give in order to be seen giving, it carries different connotations from if we give because our hearts move us to help another person. Thus, motives and attitudes are linked, according to Jesus. The manner in which we give reflects the interior reason for the giving.

Financial status was also significant for Jesus, a gift that came from well within a person's means did not require the same effort or sacrifice as a gift that was offered out of poverty. Jesus did not condemn the widow as reckless for giving everything she possessed. After all, widows were already dependent on others for their daily living, as commanded throughout the books of Exodus and Deuteronomy. Yet the poor, as well as the wealthy, still had a duty to give, and so the widow was conscientiously fulfilling her religious duty. The difference for her was that her sacrifice could be life-threatening, if others failed to provide as they ought.

What we learn from this is that, in God's eyes, the act of giving alone is not enough. In our giving, our motives can be far from altruistic, but when we make sacrifices in the name of God he will not leave us desolate. It is interesting to note that this story was the last public teaching of Jesus before his arrest and his own much more costly sacrifice.

Spiritual exercise

❖ What does this story tell you about the importance of giving and sacrifice?

❖ Reflect on your own motives for giving and receiving.

❖ How do you balance trust in God to provide for you with your duty to be a wise steward of your resources?

❖ What do you learn about your responsibilities towards the vulnerable?

Prayer

Giving God,
your Son watched the crowds
visiting the temple day after day.
The rich came to flash their wealth,
the widow shuffled her coins in poverty,
while you sat and judged them from the heart:
graceless giving is worth less than two coins of love.
Amen

Reflection

In our society we are urged both to give and to save our money in countless ways. This Lent, may we examine our motives for giving, whether in church, among family and friends or to the charities we support.

It is finished

Near the cross of Jesus stood his mother, his mother's sister, Mary the wife of Clopas, and Mary Magdalene. When Jesus saw his mother there, and the disciple whom he loved standing nearby, he said to his mother, 'Dear woman, here is your son,' and to the disciple, 'Here is your mother.' From that time on, this disciple took her into his home. Later, knowing that all was now completed, and so that the Scripture would be fulfilled, Jesus said, 'I am thirsty.' A jar of wine vinegar was there, so they soaked a sponge in it, put the sponge on a stalk of the hyssop plant, and lifted it to Jesus' lips. When he had received the drink, Jesus said, 'It is finished.' With that, he bowed his head and gave up his spirit.

JOHN 19:25–30

The climax of the passion narrative comes at Golgotha where Jesus is crucified. Although we only have a part of the whole story here, it is worth reading all of John 19 to grasp the full extent of the suffering of Jesus' last hours.

John's emphasis on the triumphant initiative of Jesus, even in his darkest moment, continues. There is no Simon of Cyrene pressurised into carrying the cross, as in the other Gospel accounts. In John's Gospel (19:17), Jesus carries it himself: perhaps this suggests that, for John, Jesus was still in charge of his own fate.

The moment of crucifixion is a mock enthronement: Jesus is crucified between two other men who die in the same way but for different crimes. Over Jesus' head is written, in Aramaic, Latin and Greek, 'Jesus of Nazareth, the King of the Jews'. Even though the chief priests protest, Pilate is adamant that this will be the official title of the crucified Jesus, unwittingly affirming both the truth that Jesus' opponents desperately sought to reject and the global nature of his sacrifice, as the inscription could be read by Jews, Romans and Greeks.

Earlier in this Gospel, John cites the haunting symbolism of the bronze serpent as described in Numbers 21:6–9 (see John 3:14). The Israelites were asked to look at a poisonous snake, an image of the cause of their despair. In order to be healed, they had to confront the thing that they feared. John's Gospel presents the crucifixion as a similar 'lifting up'—not just the physical raising of the crucified body of Jesus in mortal agony, but a triumphant exaltation. By being lifted up, Jesus, as the Word made flesh, completes his mission of love and returns to the Father—and through him we are healed.

John fills this climactic death scene with other potent symbols. The seamless tunic of Jesus, which is not torn, and about which Psalm 22:18 graphically prophesied, is reminiscent of the high priest's robe, and it may represent the unity that Jesus came to create. It could also be read as an echo of Joseph's unifying coat, which we considered in our reflections on forgiveness, or of the seamless curtain veil in the temple, which featured in our reflections on holiness. On the brink of death, Jesus' physical and spiritual thirst recalls his words to Peter in the garden: 'Shall I not drink the cup the Father has given me?' (John 18:11).

John's Gospel deliberately mentions episodes not found in the other Gospels. Jesus' words to his mother and 'the beloved disciple' are found only here. (Traditionally the 'beloved disciple' is assumed to be John, the brother of James and the author of this Gospel or the material on which it was based.) Although Mary and John were not closely related to each other, and this arrangement could not have been legally binding, they were united in their deep love of Jesus and in their shock and grief.

The symbolic meaning of this incident is difficult to determine. It might mean that the beloved disciple is now a member of Jesus' household or community; or that Jesus' mother, symbolising Judaism, now gives birth to a new community symbolised by Jesus' beloved disciple. This would bridge the gap between the newly emerging Christian community and its heritage in Judaism, thus commanding respect for Christianity's roots. There is one clear message that John wants us to grasp here, however: John and Mary were bound together by their relationship with Jesus rather than by natural ties. Through Jesus Christ—through his death and resurrection—we who believe are also bound together as one new family, and our spiritual bonds are as strong as, if not stronger than, our blood relationships. John and Mary created a new relationship through Jesus. If the cross does not unite us, what will?

John describes the death of Jesus succinctly. Jesus' last words are 'It is finished' (v. 30). The Greek verb used here implies 'completion' and 'arriving at the intended goal'. From the start, Jesus had set out to do the will of his Father and to love humanity until the bitter end. No one has stolen his life; he has given it willingly. He is freely obedient and obediently free. In consequence, we see the horror of death defused by Jesus' compassion for his closest family and friends, coupled with an outpouring of his universal and perfect love.

Spiritual exercise

❖ What do Jesus' words to Mary say to you about his relationship with his mother?

❖ What is the significance of Jesus' sacrifice for your own faith?

❖ Reflect on sacrifices you have made, whether freely given or not. Have they deepened your relationship with God?

❖ What does Jesus mean by 'It is finished' and how does this relate to your life?

Prayer

Giving God,
you gave us everything
but we raised you high on a cross.
We called you 'King of the Jews',
yet we nailed you as a criminal.
We cast lots for your clothing
but you crowned us with seamless love.
Amen

Reflection

There is no quick or easy way to understand Christ's
death or, indeed, any death. This Lent, however, we can
remember that through Christ's perfect sacrifice we have
been saved.

Only a shadow

First he said, 'Sacrifices and offerings, burnt offerings and sin offerings you did not desire, nor were you pleased with them' (although the law required them to be made). Then he said, 'Here I am, I have come to do your will.' He sets aside the first to establish the second. And by that will, we have been made holy through the sacrifice of the body of Jesus Christ once for all. Day after day every priest stands and performs his religious duties; again and again he offers the same sacrifices, which can never take away sins. But when this priest had offered for all time one sacrifice for sins, he sat down at the right hand of God. Since that time he waits for his enemies to be made his footstool, because by one sacrifice he has made perfect forever those who are being made holy.

HEBREWS 10:8–14

The letter to the Hebrews states that Jesus Christ is both the perfect priest and the perfect sacrifice. The Greek word for 'perfect' could also be translated as 'complete': we are completely forgiven by Christ, completely cleansed, and therefore perfectly qualified to worship God, perfectly able to have a relationship with him. One of the weaknesses of the sacrificial system was the need for repeated sacrifices; this repetition demonstrated their inefficacy. Jesus' sacrifice was fully and finally effective and therefore did not have to be re-enacted again and again.

In verse 1 of Hebrews 10, the law is described as 'only a shadow of the good things that are coming'. The word 'shadow' is not used to denote a contrast between light and darkness so much as to express a foretelling, a foreshadowing of that which is to come in Christ. Just as the tabernacle was a copy of God's presence in heaven, so also the rituals of sacrifice were shadows of the real sacrifice of Jesus Christ. The tabernacle and its rituals symbolised good things but could not bring them about. The law often talked about cleansing and forgiveness, but, in and of itself, it could not cleanse or forgive. No matter how many animals were killed, no matter how many offerings were made, the law could never achieve the forgiveness that the new covenant now offered to all believers.

The author of the letter to the Hebrews thus clearly summarised the argument against the old covenant system: the sacrifices, instead of cleansing the people, were really an annual reminder of sins, because it was impossible for the blood of bulls and goats to take away people's sins. A physical substance, such as blood, could not remove a spiritual mark. The Old Testament saints were forgiven their sins, but this was done on the basis of faith and God's grace, not because they had paid a big enough price or had earned forgiveness. The sacrifices reflected a shadow of forgiveness: they referred to forgiveness but they were not the means to gain forgiveness. Jesus came to bridge the gap between heaven and earth, between spirit and matter, in a way that nothing and no one else could. Only he could make an offering on earth that was truly acceptable to his Father in heaven. The actual flesh and blood of his body were no different from the flesh and blood of any other crucified man, but they were made effective for our sanctification and our forgiveness because Jesus was perfectly obedient to his Father's will.

In our reflections on holiness, we read how the high priest alone had access to the Most Holy Place of the temple. In the Old Testament, the concepts of holiness and sacrifice were clearly defined by the idea of separation. Separation between God and humankind, with the high priest as mediator, shaped the faith and worship of the Israelites. Here in Hebrews, we are told that because Jesus has now become the perfect sacrifice, the high priest is no longer a bridge offering exclusive access to God. Nor do the priests who offer endless sacrifices still possess a special power. For the first time in history, through Jesus' sacrificial death, rather than being excluded from the Most Holy Place, we are all invited in.

Spiritual exercise

❖ What might the word 'shadow' mean in terms of your own faith?

❖ Reflect on some religious rituals in your own life and what they mean to you.

❖ How are you made holy through Jesus' perfect sacrifice?

❖ Reflect on how it feels to be invited into the Most Holy Place—into God's presence.

Prayer

Giving God,
We brought you sacrifice after sacrifice
but these were only shadows of the truth.
We made the same offerings again and again,
but they could not cancel our debts.
You came among us in flesh and blood;
your perfect love made us holy for ever.
Amen

Reflection

The letter to the Hebrews urges us to accept the perfect offering of Jesus and to be forgiven. This Lent, let us confess our sins, offer contrite hearts and live not in the shadows but in the Christ-light.

✤

Hope

*Faith has to do with things that are not seen, and hope
with things that are not in hand.*

ST THOMAS AQUINAS, FROM *SUMMA THEOLOGICA* (1264–74)

~~~~~~

One of the most profound themes running through
the passion narratives is that of hope. If it were not
for hope, much of the agony and suffering of Christ
would appear to have been in vain. During Lent and
Easter, we usually emphasise the details of Jesus' dying
on the cross and his rising from death on the third day.
The middle day is often overlooked. Is Holy Saturday
just a time of limbo before the main point, the final
victory? It's as if the world is waiting: as time stops,
God stops, love stops and silence blankets the earth.
Holy Saturday teaches us much about hope.

We make a mistake if we think of the passage between Good Friday and Easter Day as simply a route
from A to B; our salvation does not consist of escape
from death or life on the other side of death. Rather,
the victory passes through death.

The death of Jesus took place according to the will
of God made known in the Old Testament (Numbers 24:17; Isaiah 53; Zechariah 12:10). Between the
sixth and ninth hours, darkness covered the earth.

Jesus uttered a cry and breathed his last. The temple curtain dividing the Holy Place from the Holy of Holies (Exodus 26:33) was torn apart, ending the old covenant with Israel. Jesus' cry of abandonment in Matthew 27:45–46 and Mark 15:34, 'My God, my God, why have you forsaken me?', comes from Psalm 22. We should remember, though, that this is not simply a cry of despair but proof of the fulfilment of the psalm's prediction of Jesus' death. It is also the cry of a man who, in that moment, felt his imminent submission to death as both human and divine, and therefore knew that he could not be saved from it. It was his destiny. What died was perishable, weak and mortal; what rose is imperishable, glorious and immortal.

What we see in Jesus' death is not a pointless suffering but a completed suffering, and in that completed suffering we pass from the events of Good Friday to the silence of Holy Saturday. If Good Friday represents Jesus' self-surrender, Holy Saturday symbolises his identification with us even in absolute helplessness. On this day we remember Jesus suspended between times, awaiting resurrection.

Holy Saturday is the reconciliation of this extraordinary moment between death and resurrection. To understand this between-time, this hiatus, we need to bear in mind the concept of Sheol—the Hebrew name for the realm of the dead, which was the exact opposite of everything the nation of Israel understood about God. God is the God of the living, the Creator God. By contrast, Sheol is the pit, the land of darkness cut off from communication with the living. By his death,

Jesus enters into the experience of the lifeless passivity of Sheol and shows that even that place is not beyond the reach of the love and power of God.

So what can we learn from reflecting on the between-time? On Holy Saturday it is too early to think of triumph. We can only wait and hope—but isn't life more often about waiting and hoping, holding one's breath, than it is about spiritual highs or lows? Many are the ordinary days when little happens that is different. The Holy Saturdays of our lives have much to teach us because, if we are unable to be patient and hopeful but remain distracted, questioning and searching, we have missed the point of the importance of waiting. It is only in waiting that we learn how to be ready to move on.

Between conception and birth there are nine months; between youth and old age there are plenty of years; between innocence and wisdom there are many experiences. Life is made up of stages and sometimes we need something crucial to happen in our faith journey to allow us to move on to the next stage. At other times, life appears slow and unpromising—yet these times can offer real opportunities for inner trans-formation. The challenge is in balancing the tension between movement and pause. The Holy Saturday times can make all the difference to us. How often do we fail to see the red light because we're too busy looking for the green? How often do we push a door that says 'pull' because we're so keen to get out? The world crowds in on us but we have a choice to be still, to stop and to wait.

We don't need to rush it.

Make yourself an ark

'So make yourself an ark of cypress wood; make rooms in it and coat it with pitch inside and out. This is how you are to build it: the ark is to be 450 feet long, 75 feet wide and 45 feet high. Make a roof for it and finish the ark to within 18 inches of the top. Put a door in the side of the ark and make lower, middle and upper decks. I am going to bring floodwaters on the earth to destroy all life under the heavens, every creature that has the breath of life in it. Everything on earth will perish. But I will establish my covenant with you, and you will enter the ark—you and your sons and your wife and your sons' wives with you. You are to bring into the ark two of all living creatures, male and female, to keep them alive with you. Two of every kind of bird, of every kind of animal and of every kind of creature that moves along the ground will come to you to be kept alive. You are to take every kind of food that is to be eaten and store it away as food for you and for them.' Noah did everything just as God commanded him.
GENESIS 6:14–22

The biblical story begins in Genesis with two accounts of a loving, creative God forming the earth and bringing humanity into being. This story concludes in Revelation with this same God reigning over a healing community that becomes the new and glorious home all this space for themselves, but, before God explains to Noah the relevance of his design, he describes the ark's wider purpose: 'I will establish my covenant with you' (v. 18). This is often seen as prefiguring God's covenant with Noah, described in Genesis 9:9–17. Here, however, God talks about establishing the covenant, and not making it. It may well be, therefore, that this is a reference to an older promise, made to Eve in the garden of Eden, that through her will come the Messiah. This promise of a future Messiah can be seen in God's rebuke of Satan (Genesis 3:15). It is firstly a promise of destruction for the serpent, and only secondly the promise of salvation for Adam and Eve and the whole human race. The Messiah was to come, then, both to destroy Satan and to deliver humanity from his dominion—a theme that, as we know, continues throughout the New Testament. In Genesis 6, God confirms that the covenant will still be fulfilled as promised and that the line will continue through Noah's family. It is important to observe that Noah was not taken out of the judgment; rather, he was to be saved through it. God provided him with a miraculous shelter from the wrath of his judgment upon the world.

We return to God's grief, which stemmed from his sense of loss. God felt broken when his creation was broken; he is portrayed not as an impersonal judge but as a friend betrayed. Out of his deep grief for the world that he had made with his own hands comes the flood. The chaos that had been unified at the beginning of creation (Genesis 2:1–4) now returns to chaos once more. The destroying waters rise and the flood wreaks devastation. Only the tiny remnant of Noah, his family and the animals on the ark will remain, because God cannot bear to destroy everything. He wants to save something. What we observe here is the tension that humans perceive in the character of God, and the tensions that we struggle to live with in ourselves—namely, the tension between righteousness and justice, and love and mercy.

The story goes on to tell how the waters subside (8:10–12). Chaos recedes. God recreates. God blesses Noah and affirms that human beings are still in God's image, restoring their dominion over the rest of creation (9:1–7). He gives back the responsibility of stewardship, the responsibility to care for the broken world. Then the narrative ends in 9:11 with God's heartfelt promise: 'Never again will there be a flood to destroy the earth.' The depths of God's mercy are revealed and his love poured out.

Of course we know that in the history of Israel, the people continued to disobey God, destroy his creation and destroy themselves. In the end, though, these events led neither to the Spirit of God hovering over the primal waters nor just Noah and his ark, floating above the depths, hoping and waiting for dry land. Rather, they point towards the ultimate Saviour—Christ Jesus, whose own blood will be poured out for the world.

It is hope in God that rises from these dark, early waters of faith towards the wellspring of faith with his Son's coming on earth.

Spiritual exercise

❖ What does the ark symbolise for you about Christian faith?

❖ Imagine you are Mrs Noah in this story. What emotions might you feel?

❖ What does this story teach us about God's creation and its hope for survival?

❖ What images of God do you think are evoked here?

Prayer

God of hope,
you flooded your earth with the waters of your grief.
You set Noah, his family and all the animals apart
in an ark of promise and salvation.
You destroyed what you had made,
but the dove returned holding an olive twig,
and your covenant remained.
Amen

Reflection

The flood was God's judgment upon the earth but he saved a few in an ark. This Lent, seek God's saving shelter by placing your faith and hope in him alone.

My soul waits

Out of the depths I cry to you, O Lord; O Lord, hear my voice. Let your ears be attentive to my cry for mercy. If you, O Lord, kept a record of sins, O Lord, who could stand? But with you there is forgiveness; therefore you are feared. I wait for the Lord, my soul waits, and in his word I put my hope. My soul waits for the Lord more than watchmen wait for the morning, more than watchmen wait for the morning. O Israel, put your hope in the Lord, for with the Lord is unfailing love and with him is full redemption. He himself will redeem Israel from all their sins.

PSALM 130

This is a wonderful psalm because of the way it speaks of God's offer of forgiveness through grace, quite apart from our need to earn it. It is also known as the *De Profundis*, from the Latin for the first four words, and has been set to music by numerous composers including Bach, Handel, Mozart, Mendelssohn and Rutter. It has also inspired many writers throughout history, including C.S. Lewis, Christina Rossetti and Oscar Wilde.

The structure of this psalm follows a formula: lament; confession of sin; waiting for the Lord; confidence in redemption. It is a penitential psalm, starting at the lowest depths of despair and progressing steadily upwards until, at the end, there is a sense of confidence, encouragement and total trust in God. It is part of a series of 15 psalms (120—134) known as the 'songs of ascent', probably because they were sung by pilgrims processing up to Jerusalem. Interestingly, their verses share a characteristic movement from the abyss of depression to the high ground of steadfast hope.

The psalm switches from talking to Yahweh to talking about Yahweh, and then talks to Israel about waiting for redemption from Yahweh. The author not only pleads his own case before Yahweh, but also pleads for Israel to trust in Yahweh's love and redemption, and so we move from a personal to a collective response. The psalmist starts by saying that he cries out from the 'depths', which could be read as a reference to the depths of the sea. To the ancient Israelites, the sea symbolised chaos, mystery and terror —even death—because it could not be mastered by humanity. (Compare Noah building the ark, a vessel that would withstand the destructive power of the flood.) The psalmist uses this metaphor to suggest that he is overwhelmed by his problems, just as someone would feel if they were drowning in deep waters. The depths in which he suffers have separated him from his God, causing him to cry out with a sense of rejection and loneliness.

This terrible plight, the psalmist's sense of alienation, arouses our compassion and we feel his pain, anguish and utter dependence on God. Verse 3, referring to human sinfulness, is a rhetorical question and is not, therefore, intended to receive an answer. The psalmist realises that if God were to monitor our sins, no one would be good enough to stand before him. The idea that God records our sins is not unique to this verse: it is also found in Deuteronomy 32:34 and Hosea 13:12.

This psalm speaks directly to us about those times in our lives when we also find ourselves in 'the depths'. The real question is what we do, once we realise that we are in those depths. The psalmist urges us to wait patiently for God to help us (vv. 5–6). Often we don't wait long enough: we don't make time to be with God and listen to him. We don't like waiting but, with God, this is what we have to do. We are not waiting because God is too busy with other things and other people, but because we are not ready to be in his presence and hear him. If we look at it another way, it is God who is waiting for us. One meaning of the Hebrew word translated here as 'wait' is 'to bind together', as if with a strong rope. We have to bind ourselves together with God. We have to allow ourselves to become one with God, to reach the point where we can hardly tell where we finish and God begins. This takes much time and space—a whole lifetime, in fact.

Another interpretation of the word 'depths' points towards its ultimate meaning: the word is often used to indicate either space or profundity. What do we mean when we say that our suffering is 'deep'? Perhaps it is to do with the depths of our thoughts and experiences—the depths of our sense of meaning in life. Naturally we want answers to make sense of this deep meaning, and the search for such answers requires listening rather than just questioning. Our problem is that we are always wanting and waiting for things in the

Reflection

Being in the depths of despair and waiting in hope are particularly difficult aspects of our life, but Psalm 130 assures us that, through them, we will find God. This Lent, let us trust God in our sorrows, whatever they are, by allowing his infinite love to fill our souls.

Set your hope

Concerning this salvation, the prophets, who spoke of the grace that was to come to you, searched intently and with the greatest care, trying to find out the time and circumstances to which the Spirit of Christ in them was pointing when he predicted the sufferings of Christ and the glories that would follow. It was revealed to them that they were not serving themselves but you, when they spoke of the things that have now been told you by those who have preached the gospel to you by the Holy Spirit sent from heaven. Even angels long to look into these things. Therefore, prepare your minds for action; be self-controlled; set your hope fully on the grace to be given you when Jesus Christ is revealed. As obedient children, do not conform to the evil desires you had when you lived in ignorance. But just as he who called you is holy, so be holy in all you do; for it is written: 'Be holy, because I am holy.'

1 PETER 1:10–16

The first letter of Peter was written to both Jewish and Gentile Christians, spread throughout Asia Minor, who faced persecution for their newly expressed faith. If Hebrews is the letter of faith, and 1 Corinthians and 1 John the letters of love, then we see that 1 Peter is clearly the letter of hope.

While suffering is a prevailing theme in 1 Peter, the apostle offers hope as its counterpoint. It is hope that gives all Christians real encouragement in the midst of their daily tribulations. Hope enables us to focus more directly on the blessings that we have been promised rather than simply on our circumstances here and now. We are given something that goes beyond today or tomorrow and reaches to eternity.

Like faith, hope is a response to God's goodness and free grace. At the same time, hope is also an aspect of our relationship with God and, therefore, has corresponding implications for the way we live out our faith. Peter commands us to be holy and steadfast in our behaviour: we are not to be defeated by our sufferings or distracted by competing ideologies or political powers. Rather, we need to live in and through God for his glory. This requirement to be obedient is not intended to oppress our personalities and preferences, but to enable us to find a new freedom in serving the one God consistently and with our whole hearts.

Peter's letter is very practical: it does not avoid the difficulties and hardships that believers face. Christians are urged to do good, to imitate Christ and to practise what they preach, regardless of whether they are heard or dismissed by their audience. One of the most basic commands found in scripture is to be holy because the Lord our God is holy (see Leviticus 11:44–45; 19:2; 20:7). Since Christians follow Christ, they should naturally reflect his holiness in their living. This is not simply an individual call for each Christian but a calling to the global community of faith. This community should reflect Christ's holiness in its entirety and within the mutual relationships that make it up.

Peter wants to encourage Christians who suffer for the sake of their faith because, although they will suffer in this life (and this suffering is unavoidable), they will not suffer for ever. This world is passing. Heaven is our destination, where one day we will live with God and share in his glory. Peter also wants his readers to understand what God has done for them. He wants them to learn more about the beauty and the creative acts of God, his Son's sacrifice on the cross and his resurrection. Once we realise the extent of God's love and grace, Peter believes, we will feel more gratitude and wonder about our salvation.

Drawing on the prophets and the angels who prepared the way for the Messiah as messengers, protectors and intermediaries between God and his people, Peter claims that they also longed to see what we have now experienced through the gospel of Jesus Christ. Starting in the garden of Eden, angels guarded the tree of life; Abraham, Hagar, Jacob, Moses and many of the prophets encountered angels telling them what they should do. The prophet Zechariah received eight visions from angels, while many of the psalms mention angels as defenders and protectors and as worshippers of God. Their fervour in past eras should encourage us in hope and zeal to stay close to God, no matter what we face. If we set our hope on God, he will not fail us.

✛

Spiritual exercise

❖ What words from Peter's letter speak to you most today?

❖ How might you reflect God's holiness in your own life?

❖ Have you ever felt persecuted for your faith?

❖ How does grace strengthen you in your relationship with God?

Prayer

God of hope,
your prophets foretold your grace
and yearned to see it revealed in Christ.
They served you long ago in faith and truth
so that we might join them in future glory.
Help us to be holy for you
and await your second coming with hopeful hearts.
Amen

Reflection

Hope involves a relationship with the person in whom the hope is placed. This Lent, may we kneel at the cross and, in humble gratitude, accept our responsibility of receiving Christ's grace, which comes from his loving sacrifice.

The fullness of God

For this reason I kneel before the Father, from whom his whole family in heaven and on earth derives its name. I pray that out of his glorious riches he may strengthen you with power through his Spirit in your inner being, so that Christ may dwell in your hearts through faith. And I pray that you, being rooted and established in love, may have power, together with all the saints, to grasp how wide and long and high and deep is the love of Christ, and to know this love that surpasses knowledge—that you may be filled to the measure of all the fullness of God. Now to him who is able to do immeasurably more than all we ask or imagine, according to his power that is at work within us, to him be glory in the church and in Christ Jesus throughout all generations, for ever and ever! Amen.

EPHESIANS 3:14–21

The letter to the Christian community at Ephesus, one of the most important bases for the expansion of the faith, is concerned with uniting the church in its fellowship and hope and in the necessary requirements for living as Christians. Like most of the New Testament letters, it emphasises the application of the faith in the daily lives of believers and urges trust in the God in whom they should believe. Ephesians has sometimes been described as the quintessence of Pauline theology because of its grace-centred focus and its references to the Holy Spirit's power and gifts. Although it is not certain that Paul wrote Ephesians, this is highly likely to be the case, given its similarities to, and development of, themes found in his other letters.

The first three chapters of Ephesians, from which today's reading is taken, use the language of prayer and praise to renew and inspire Christians in their faith. In prayer and worship, we often kneel as a sign of reverence before God. When we kneel, we have a different visual perspective from when we sit or stand. In a similar way, this letter provides us with the opportunity to see the world differently, from an attitude of humility before God. As Paul kneels and speaks directly to his readers, he encourages us also to kneel in prayer and praise.

Our reading begins abruptly with 'For this reason…' This phrase refers to what Paul has been saying in previous paragraphs about his ministry. Paul, like all the other apostles, had been entrusted with sharing the faith through, and by, the Spirit. God had also revealed to him that the Gentiles who received the gospel in faith were equal to the Jewish Christians and fellow heirs, with them, of the promises of God. They were equal members of the body of Christ and therefore had equal access to God. Thus it is 'For this reason…' that the author prays that his readers will be strengthened with spiritual power, love and knowledge of God.

A closer look at the prayer's content reveals four requests:

- Spiritual strength
- The rooting and indwelling of Christ in the believers' hearts
- The ability to understand the spiritual dimensions of the Christian faith
- Knowledge and authentic experience of the love of Christ.

God's love and power are broader, deeper, wider and taller than the dimensions of all the other physical realities in our universe. That is to say, God is far greater than that which he has created. Knowing the love of Christ is greater than knowledge itself.

In this letter, Paul describes the beauty of a multi-dimensional God, who is a God of power (Ephesians 1:19), generous in mercy (2:4), lavish in his grace (2:7; 3:7) and infinite in his wisdom (3:10). In our reading today, Paul's prayer finishes with a doxology or hymn of praise that gives glory to God (vv. 20–21). This glory dwells 'in the church and in Christ Jesus'. Thus it is present within all believers in union with Christ, who is glorified in God. Such glory is possible because the church is Christ's very body (see Ephesians 1:23; 4:15–16; 5:30). Christ and his church are deeply and intimately one. All Christians who are members of the church through their faith and baptism are also united with Christ, in God.

Paul addresses the Ephesians as a corporate body and not as individual believers. The four spiritual qualities for which he prayed earlier are to be found, developed and nurtured within the corporate body of the church. While these qualities are undoubtedly important for each individual, they are particularly appropriate for the church as a whole. Most of us are strengthened and sustained by the witness of the company of fellow believers. Our mutual participation in the life of the church nurtures and challenges our faith and offers the world a sign of our collective faith.

The indwelling of Christ in the hearts of believers is the means by which love is created and developed. Christ is not just a distant memory or a historical figure; we do not have to somehow conjure up his presence. He comes to us in word, sacrament and relationship whenever we ask him. Where Christ is, there is perfect love until the time when we will see him face to face in glory—and that is our perfect hope.

Spiritual exercise

❖ If you are able to, kneel as you pray today. If not, reflect on what praying in a different bodily position reveals to you about God.
❖ Where do you most find hope in this passage from Ephesians?
❖ How might you nurture your inner being?
❖ If God's love surpasses knowledge, where, or with whom, could you share this love?

Prayer

God of hope,
as I kneel before you in humble prayer
and stretch out my hands in praise,
the dimensions of your love transcend this world.
You dwell in my heart and take root in my soul;
your presence fills me beyond measure.
In you alone I have power from above.
Amen

Reflection

Throughout all generations the power of the Holy Spirit reveals God's glory. This Lent, pray that the Holy Spirit will dwell in your heart and that your church may be filled with the fullness of God.

A new heaven and a new earth

Then I saw a new heaven and a new earth, for the first heaven and the first earth had passed away, and there was no longer any sea. I saw the Holy City, the new Jerusalem, coming down out of heaven from God, prepared as a bride beautifully dressed for her husband. And I heard a loud voice from the throne saying, 'Now the dwelling of God is with men, and he will live with them. They will be his people, and God himself will be with them and be their God. He will wipe every tear from their eyes. There will be no more death or mourning or crying or pain, for the old order of things has passed away.'

REVELATION 21:1–4

The last book in the Christian Bible is known both as Revelation, from the Latin *revelatio* (an unveiling or revealing of the truth hidden behind an appearance), and as the Apocalypse, from the Greek *apokalypsis* (an uncovering). Revelation belongs to that body of literature in which a prophet or seer experiences and describes symbolic visions about the future, the heavens and the end time. There is much dispute about the authorship of Revelation because, although it is attributed to 'John', it is very different in style, language and thought from John's Gospel and the Johannine letters.

Revelation is simultaneously about the 'now' and the time still to come. It holds the past, present and future in a vivid and extraordinary balance. It emphasises faith in and through suffering, the final triumphant victory of God over Satan and the powers of darkness, and confident hope in Jesus' return as the spotless sacrificial Lamb of God. Its use of creative imagination, fantasy and highly complex symbolism provides an inexhaustible richness of language and purpose that numerous writers and artists have sought to interpret for their own time.

The message of Revelation is about both an impending crisis, of which the churches seem to be wholly unaware, and a promise of the total defeat of evil through Christ. Three sets of disasters are laid out—war, death and famine—which are paralleled by corresponding liberation through God as the creator, redeemer and renewer of heaven and earth. Although John never quotes directly from any other book in the Bible, he alludes to much of the Old Testament, notably Genesis, Exodus, the Psalms and the prophets, especially Daniel.

In Revelation 21, John begins to describe the promised age to come, when Satan and his armies have been defeated and the whole of humanity has been judged. Those who are saved now live in the presence of God for ever and in perfect peace. The true glory of this age will be greater than we can ever imagine, because it will supersede all that this earth can offer us. We should approach the final two chapters of Revelation with a sense of hope, humility and wonder at God's promise.

The formal idea of a new heaven and a new earth also occurs in Isaiah 65:17; 66:22 and 2 Peter 3:13, and it is implied in Isaiah 51:6; Matthew 19:28; 2 Corinthians 5:17 and Hebrews 12:26–28. The adjective 'new' describes not so much a world that is entirely different from what we experience now, but one that is new in its quality. This new world will be better than anything we have encountered previously; it will be a supreme form of the world we have now, because it will be wherever we dwell with God.

The Old Testament had no single word for 'universe', so the phrase 'heaven and earth' serves to encompass this meaning. The promise of 'a new heaven and a new earth' is therefore equivalent to a promise of total cosmic renewal. John uses the analogy of a marriage to illustrate the relationship between this new world and its Creator. It is a marriage between the glorified Christ as bridegroom and his bride, the Church—all of us who believe in him. The old order with its rules and parameters will be stripped away because it is no longer relevant, and Christ will restore universal harmony at last. Our hope in an invisible God will become a living reality in a visible God.

Spiritual exercise

❖ Can you imagine a world where there is no more death or pain?

Love

*Christian love is not the world's last word about itself—
it is God's final word about himself, and so about the
world.*

HANS URS VON BALTHASAR, FROM *LOVE ALONE: THE WAY OF REVELATION*
(SHEED AND WARD, 1968)

We come to Holy Week—the week of pure love, a week
that is filled with mystery for its spectators and glory in
the suffering of its King. The cross is an enigma because
it contradicts everything we know about justice and
love, yet, in and through the cross, we best understand
God's love and God's love is made complete. Only in
and through the cross can Jesus rise from the dead
and win our eternal salvation. When love enters a
sinful world, the only way Jesus can reveal his truth is
through his own suffering. God loves us because we
are the people for whom his Son has suffered in love.

So what do we mean by love? How is love revealed
and perceived? For Christians, the most helpful starting
point for our understanding lies in Christ. In Christ, all
creation finds its fulfilment. In Christ, all of creation is
saved. Yet Christ's identity, both as a child and as an
adult, was and is frequently misunderstood. We see
this in the fear of Herod and Pilate (Matthew 2:13–18;

27:24–26), in the religious leaders in the temple who continually challenged his teachings (Mark 12:13–40; Luke 6:1–11), and in the crowds who sent him to his death, yet saved the thief Barabbas (John 18:38–40). When power is aligned with love, it can lose its potential for the free gift of self. We notice, therefore, that Christ always revealed his identity in relation to his Father, never in his own right. His will was his Father's will.

Jesus appeared to turn the world, as the Jewish people knew it, upside down with his challenging messages about the Law, justice, poverty, righteousness, forgiveness and healing. He presented the scriptures, familiar as they were, in a new light and drew out layers of meaning previously unseen, yet the people still did not grasp his truths. For Jesus, therefore, the only way he could show the world the truth was in and through his perfect, sacrificial love.

Jesus was an expert in relationships. He healed the sick; he was master and servant, friend and king. Jesus loved people in a way they had never experienced before—but he also needed to be on his own from time to time, to pray for the world, for those who persecuted him, for those who believed in him, for the lost and the weary, the oppressed and forgotten, and for those who were alone. Jesus sat with prostitutes and Pharisees and loved them equally, although he had different things to say to them. There was no one he did not accept, no one he couldn't embrace.

In Jesus we experience complete love. Even when he ascended to his Father after the resurrection, he ensured that the Holy Spirit would guide and protect his people; he did not abandon us. There is nothing that he overlooks and nothing he forgets to do. All that is now left is for him to return. Until that time, we live and die in his grace-filled gift of love.

One another's feet

He came to Simon Peter, who said to him, 'Lord, are you going to wash my feet?' Jesus replied, 'You do not realise now what I am doing, but later you will understand.' 'No,' said Peter, 'you shall never wash my feet.' Jesus answered, 'Unless I wash you, you have no part with me.' … When he had finished washing their feet, he put on his clothes and returned to his place. 'Do you understand what I have done for you?' he asked them. 'You call me "Teacher" and "Lord", and rightly so, for that is what I am. Now that I, your Lord and Teacher, have washed your feet, you also should wash one another's feet. I have set you an example that you should do as I have done for you. I tell you the truth, no servant is greater than his master, nor is a messenger greater than the one who sent him. Now that you know these things, you will be blessed if you do them.'

JOHN 13:6–8, 12–17

Shortly after Jesus and his friends had celebrated Passover together, Jesus rose from the table and began washing his friends' feet. Why was this significant? Unlike many other Jewish rituals, foot-washing was not primarily a ceremonial custom. It was important because people walked in sandals or barefoot through dusty and dirty streets. To wash someone else's feet was regarded as one of the most demeaning tasks that anyone could perform and, not surprisingly, was reserved for household slaves. At this Passover meal, there appeared to be no slaves present, so who was going to carry out this menial task?

How could Jesus, the disciples' Lord and Master, possibly sink so low as to wash dirty human feet? The disciples could have washed their own feet, which is what often happened in the absence of a servant. For Jesus to step in was nothing short of a scandal. Unlike some of the other outrageous and incomprehensible acts that they had seen Jesus commit—speaking out against the Pharisees, challenging deep-rooted injustices, conversing freely with children and women, tax collectors and prostitutes, and healing on the sabbath— the disciples genuinely couldn't see how this enhanced their understanding of Jesus and his message. Yet it is precisely in the washing of their feet that Jesus personifies service and equality.

First of all, Jesus is not merely urging Peter to observe basic hygiene. He tells him that there is a spiritual significance to this simple task, which Peter will not understand until 'later'—that is, after Jesus' death. As Jesus carefully and calmly lays aside his garments and assumes the role of a domestic servant to wash his disciples' feet, so he also lays aside his divine status to serve those whom he loves. He will later have his garments forcefully removed from him when he lays down his life on the cross, and he himself will lay the grave clothes aside as he rises from the dead.

Secondly, Jesus is insistent: the disciples have to let him wash their feet. Unless they allow Jesus to wash away their dirt, they cannot have real fellowship with him—and it is the same for all of us. Peter's protest is unacceptable to Jesus and shows clearly that he does not know his Master properly. Jesus responds by illustrating two kinds of washing. He speaks first of the physical need for cleansing and then of the spiritual truth: we are dirty before God because we sin and we cannot cleanse ourselves. This spiritual 'washing' will make the disciples totally clean (compare Isaiah 1:18 and Psalm 103:10–12), and they need to be washed in this way only once. Peter and the other disciples have already received this type of washing by believing in Jesus as the Messiah. Peter's point of resistance may be a refusal to trust or submit fully to Jesus' leadership, it may be a refusal to admit his need for cleansing, or it may be his fear of the implications if his Master is reversing prevailing rules. What would this mean for Peter? Whose feet would *he* now have to clean?

At the same time, the disciples need to continue to allow Jesus to wash their feet. This refers to another kind of washing, which we all need in order to maintain our relationship with Jesus. We need to be purified from the ongoing effects of sin. When we turn away from God, we need to be cleansed again as we return to him.

This story is pivotal in our Christian journey, as it challenges our pride, our identity and our vision of right relationships. It reverses the obsession with 'I' and instead forces us to bend low in service to any who come our way. To imitate Jesus in his foot-washing is to model loving humility towards others. If Jesus, our

Saviour, will wash another's feet, what in creation can stop us from doing the same? Only our pride, it seems.

Spiritual exercise

❖ Have you ever washed another person's feet or had your feet washed by someone else? If you have, what did it feel like? If not, imagine how it would feel.
❖ How do Jesus' actions speak to you today?
❖ What does Jesus teach you most about your church relationships?
❖ Imagine Jesus is washing your feet. What do you want to say to him?

Prayer

Loving God,
Your Son knelt down before the disciples
to wash the feet of those he cherished.
As he looked up to explain such service,
they failed to understand.
When his own feet were nailed to the wooden cross,
your heavens blessed him from on high. Amen

Reflection

Jesus calls us to wash each other's feet. During this Holy Week, whom can you serve and bless in genuine and loving humility?

I will come back

'Do not let your hearts be troubled. Trust in God; trust also in me. In my Father's house are many rooms; if it were not so, I would have told you. I am going there to prepare a place for you. And if I go and prepare a place for you, I will come back and take you to be with me that you also may be where I am. You know the way to the place where I am going.'

JOHN 14:1–4

Jesus says that believing in him and believing in God are one and the same thing. This is a complex thought for the disciples to grasp, so Jesus extends the concept further by explaining where he is now going to and where the disciples will follow him.

He describes a house that has many rooms. The actual Greek word here means 'dwelling places'. Some people remember the King James Bible's translation, 'mansions', and imagine being in a vast space. But the idea that the Father's house is made up of many rooms, not mansions, suggests a proximity to and intimacy with the Father in heaven. We are not going to be separated; we are going to be together. We are not just going to be in the same city; we are going to be in the same house.

Christ had previously spoken to his disciples as

one who was about to leave them. The disciples were naturally sorrowful at the news of his departure and felt the threat of abandonment. So here he comforts them with the news that there is not only room for him, but room for them also. The friendship and loving closeness that Jesus wants to continue having with the disciples after his death is staggering in its beauty.

The symbolism of the many rooms has been a matter for speculation for years. It might mean that there is sufficient and suitable accommodation for every type of person in the world; the mercy of God is great enough to invite all people. This, of course, is a great challenge to us: while it means that we ourselves can gain entry, it also means that everyone else can, whatever their sins. If we can receive mercy and forgiveness, then so can others.

If we remember how many people were marginalised, unloved or dismissed by the society of Jesus' time, the very suggestion that everyone would be welcome to share a home with him would have been very far removed from the disciples' way of thinking. This was yet more shocking news. Yet it also offers a model of loving unity within diversity in the home—which is what our family life can be like.

G.K. Chesterton wrote that 'the church is a house with a hundred gates and no two people enter at exactly the same angle' (*The Catholic Church and Conversion*, 1926, p. 30). The way we will face Jesus at the end time may be different from the way non-Christians will face him: maybe we are only looking at one facet of a diamond or one side of a coin. Whatever it means, we should still be very confident that our belief in Christ is true and that it is the most important thing in our lives. Until we grasp who Jesus is, we cannot understand anything else about him.

The central point in our passage today is that Jesus is the 'way' to the Father (v. 4). Throughout the Gospel we hear of Jesus' coming from the Father, revealing God, bringing new life and returning to God. Now the focus is on Jesus' role as the one who leads people to the Father. In the Old Testament, the way to God was shown by the giving of the Law and the teaching of the prophets. Our verses from John's Gospel bring out Jesus' unique fulfilment of the two roles of truth-revealer and life-giver. His unity with the Father means that he is not just a law-giver or prophet but, being God, he is the truth and therefore transcends all that is bound to this earth.

Here is a model of unity, but not duplication, between Jesus and God, Father and Son. When John speaks of Jesus as 'the way', he is not thinking of Jesus as a heavenly figure who simply brings people to God. Jesus is the revelation and agent of God; he is poised here between heaven and earth, speaking as someone in the world but no longer of it. While this chapter of John's Gospel particularly stresses the theme of Jesus' departure, there is also the consolation that one day he will take his disciples to be with him.

The disciples, who constantly reveal the depths of their misunderstanding and confusion, are utterly bewildered, yet their confusion is crucial for us as it is the means whereby Jesus reveals his 'true identity'. In his words of comfort and explanation for his friends, we hear the self-disclosure of the loving and incarnate God.

✢

Spiritual exercise

❖ Reflect on a time when you felt assured by your trust in God.
❖ Reflect on a time when you lacked trust in God.
❖ How do you respond to the generosity of Jesus' 'many rooms' imagery?
❖ How does it feel to know that Jesus is preparing a place for you?

Prayer

Loving God,
to know Jesus is to know you,
but I am so slow in following your Son.
You have prepared a place for me
and I long to be with you there now.
Until the time comes, may I be untroubled,
and make a room for you in my heart.
Amen

Reflection

To know Jesus is to know God. During this Holy Week, let us show others the way to Christ and follow him in love.

Tenderness and compassion

If you have any encouragement from being united with Christ, if any comfort from his love, if any fellowship with the Spirit, if any tenderness and compassion, then make my joy complete by being like-minded, having the same love, being one in spirit and purpose. Do nothing out of selfish ambition or vain conceit, but in humility consider others better than yourselves. Each of you should look not only to your own interests, but also to the interests of others.

PHILIPPIANS 2:1–4

Philippians was written by Paul, while he was in prison, to the Christians living in Philippi, Greece, a city in the Roman province of Macedonia. The church at Philippi was the first church that Paul founded in Europe through his preaching to women. The cloth merchant Lydia was his first convert to Christianity there (Acts 16:14–15).

Paul was concerned that the Philippians' Christian belief and mutual love should be strengthened, as they had faced persecution for their faith. This letter is filled with appreciation and encouragement for his readers but also warns them of the dangers of opposition to the faith. Again we see that fidelity to God, in both individual and community behaviour, is important for unifying and spreading the message of the gospel, especially when there is opposition. This unity can be sustained only with patient and selfless care.

Paul clearly values knowing and loving Jesus above everything else, and his missionary zeal is boundless. He longs to inspire others to stand firm no matter what befalls them, so that together they can press forward to eternal hope in God. The warmth of this pastoral relationship seeps through his letter, and this warmth, Paul says, should also characterise the Philippian Christians' relationships with each other.

Our passage comprises a call to be unified, along with the reasons for this unity, which takes the form of encouragement in Christ, comfort through love of Christ and mutual fellowship in the Spirit. The call to unity in Christ is then developed into a second call, inviting us to model the same unity in our dealings with other people. By looking out for the needs and concerns of others and treating our fellow human beings as more important than ourselves, we will be adopting Christ's model of service and humility.

The passage as a whole is based on the idea found earlier in the letter 'that the one who began a good work in you will carry it on to completion until the day of Christ Jesus' (1:6). God's work in the believers' hearts included developing tenderness, compassion, love and fellowship with one another, as well as affection and mercy. When love is mentioned in the Old Testament, it most frequently refers to God's love for his people (see Isaiah 43:4; Jeremiah 31:3), so we can probably assume that Paul is expanding the idea to mean that if Christ loves his people, then the Philippians should also learn to love one another. The more the Philippians can model their behaviour on Christ, the more they will be united in their faith and hope. If the faithful can behave with these qualities in their daily lives, they will be witnessing to Christ to those who do not as yet believe in him, and will have the crown of joy in their hearts.

Nothing is more diametrically opposed to unity and being one in spirit and purpose than selfishness or seeking one's own interests. The two attitudes of unity and selfishness cannot co-exist. One will always have to give way to the other. The term 'selfish ambition' (v. 3) implies an ugly, grasping attitude and therefore neglect of others, which leaves a whole host of hurts and pains in its wake. Except through Christ, selfishness can never be overcome in human beings. Selfish ambition stands at the heart of what it means to be a sinful person and it is a concept found seven times in the New Testament, including five times in Paul's writings (see, for example, Galatians 5:20; Philippians 1:17).

Paul says that if the Philippians are true believers, they will work together. They will love each other and they will serve each other. Paul urges them to remember Christ's death on the cross because, through his sacrifice, we have the means to imitate him in our lesser sacrifices. This model of perfect self-sacrifice is the true language of love and the means to eternal life for all believers.

✢

Spiritual exercise

❖ What does 'being one in Spirit and purpose' mean to you in your faith?
❖ How can you promote unity among the Christian brothers and sisters in your church?
❖ Reflect on a time when you acted with selfish ambition.
❖ Reflect on a time when tenderness and compassion have been shown to you.

Prayer

Loving God,
tenderness and compassion are hallmarks of your Son,
who obeyed your will by his gift of life.
When I am vain and selfish,
bring me down from the high places of pride—
to the broken hands and feet of Christ,
and humble me in the wounds of his love.
Amen

Reflection

Paul urges us to think seriously about the interests of other people. During this Holy Week, ask God to guide you in an altruistic action.

The stone had been removed

Early on the first day of the week, while it was still dark, Mary Magdalene went to the tomb and saw that the stone had been removed from the entrance. So she came running to Simon Peter and the other disciple, the one Jesus loved, and said, 'They have taken the Lord out of the tomb, and we don't know where they have put him!' So Peter and the other disciple started for the tomb. Both were running, but the other disciple outran Peter and reached the tomb first. He bent over and looked in at the strips of linen lying there but did not go in. Then Simon Peter, who was behind him, arrived and went into the tomb. He saw the strips of linen lying there, as well as the burial cloth that had been around Jesus' head. The cloth was folded up by itself, separate from the linen. Finally the other disciple, who had reached the tomb first, also went inside. He saw and believed. (They still did not understand from Scripture that Jesus had to rise from the dead.)

JOHN 20:1–9

The stone has been rolled away, the burial clothes are laid to one side and the tomb is empty, but where has Jesus gone? The Greek word for the cloth that was wrapped around Jesus' head is the same as the word used in John 11:44, in the story of the raising of Lazarus. When Lazarus emerged from the tomb, however, he was still wrapped in the cloth because he needed Jesus to revive him; Jesus needs no such catalyst. At this point, the three disciples have not encountered the risen Christ; what they have encountered is an empty tomb, the absence of Jesus and the absence of death.

Jewish tradition highly respected service and care for the dead, despite the fact that this care made the person 'unclean'. Preparing a body for burial was a cultural privilege and duty that equalled care for widows and orphans. Thus the discovery of the empty tomb took place in the context of a charitable intention by Mary Magdalene, who was coming to fulfil the last of Jesus' burial rites. Yet John adds another slant. There were two male witnesses to this event, which, in an ancient Jewish court of law, verified the fact of the case. At this moment it would have taken only a small leap of faith to conclude that Jesus had truly risen.

In John's Gospel, it is the 'other disciple', unwavering in his faith at the foot of the cross, who is the first to understand and believe after the resurrection (v. 8), then Mary Magdalene (20:14–17), then the other disciples and Thomas (vv. 19–29). Finally, Peter is singled out (21:1–23). Those who fully believed in Jesus were those who said 'yes' to him and understood the full impact of the empty tomb. Those who abandoned Jesus in his final hours were the last to come to faith. The Lord loved all who followed him completely, but the disciple who received his love and acted upon it—by not needing to enter the tomb for proof of Jesus' resurrection—was the one who first grasped the meaning of the tomb without a body.

John 20:7 tells us that the cloth that had been placed over the face of Jesus was not just lying there like the grave clothes but was neatly folded and placed separately. The folded cloth, in the Jewish tradition, was one of the symbols used in the relationship between master and servant. When the servant set the dinner table for the master, he made sure that it was exactly the way the master wanted it and placed the cloth on the table in the correct manner. Then the servant would wait, just out of sight, until the master had finished eating. If the master rose from the table, wiped his fingers and mouth and tossed the cloth on to the table, the servant would know it was time to clear the table. The cast-aside cloth meant, 'I'm done.' But if the master got up from the table, folded his cloth and laid it beside his plate, the servant would not touch the table, because the folded cloth meant, 'I'm coming back!' *Jesus is coming back!*

The resurrection of Jesus is the central mystery of our faith. In wrestling with the meaning of the resurrection, we need to avoid two extremes, however—first, seeing it only as a past event that does not really involve us now; and second, seeing it purely as something that will only happen to us after we have also died. The resurrection is a dynamic phenomenon which we Christians are constantly living through our faith in God. It is beyond time but its meaning is ever present.

The resurrection teaches us a new way of seeing the meaning of our life because it shows us how to understand death. In the resurrection, we first understand the words of the scriptures that foretold Christ's coming and the meaning of his destiny from birth to death. The resurrection unites the journey of faith between the Old and New Testaments and then takes them together into a new relationship between God and his world. It epitomises love and hope because it transcends death like nothing else on this earth. If Jesus has risen from the dead for us, he has shown us that through him we will have a new life: our own death will not be the end of our entire existence or purpose. Our physical bodies will perish but our spirit will live on in Christ. Through the resurrection, our faith opens a door to a new world.

Spiritual exercise

❖ Imagine you are running to the tomb with Mary Magdalene, Simon Peter and the other disciple. What are your thoughts right now?
❖ Where in your life does a stone need to be rolled away or a tomb opened?
❖ What does the phrase 'he saw and believed' say to your faith today?
❖ Where in your heart is your Easter joy?

Prayer

Easter Lord,
today, love and resurrection have become the perfect whole.
The tomb is empty;
Christ has risen from the dead.
Lord, help me to cherish the revelation
of your new beginning.
Today, love and resurrection have made me whole.
Amen

Reflection

Jesus has risen. Alleluia! Thank God for the miracle of the resurrection and let his love burn within you this day and always.

When he broke the bread

And beginning with Moses and all the Prophets, he explained to them what was said in all the Scriptures concerning himself. As they approached the village to which they were going, Jesus acted as if he were going farther. But they urged him strongly, 'Stay with us, for it is nearly evening; the day is almost over.' So he went in to stay with them. When he was at the table with them, he took bread, gave thanks, broke it and began to give it to them. Then their eyes were opened and they recognised him, and he disappeared from their sight. They asked each other, 'Were not our hearts burning within us while he talked with us on the road and opened the Scriptures to us?' They got up and returned at once to Jerusalem. There they found the Eleven and those with them, assembled together and saying, 'It is true! The Lord has risen and has appeared to Simon.' Then the two told what had happened on the way, and how Jesus was recognised by them when he broke the bread.

LUKE 24:27–35

Our journey in faith towards Christ is a long and rich one. It is full of pain and contradictions but also deep love and wonder. We began this Lent by considering that we are not so much waiting for Christ as accompanying him in his passion and resurrection.

The journey that we read of today, which took place after the resurrection, is not only a literal journey but also a journey in understanding more of the significance of who Christ is and what he has done.

Three days after Christ's death, two people were walking along the road to Emmaus, a village roughly seven miles from Jerusalem; one of them was called Cleopas. As they walked along, they naturally wanted to talk about the events of Jesus' death and its aftermath. Nothing like this had ever happened before, because this had been no ordinary man. So absorbed were they in their talk that they scarcely noticed when a third person drew alongside and walked with them. Jesus asked them what they were discussing and why they looked so sad.

Cleopas assumed that this man must be a stranger if he didn't know what had happened: surely everybody would know by now about Jesus' death. So the two disciples told him how Jesus had been crucified, how they had hoped that he would save Israel (which was impossible now) and how some of the faithful women they knew had gone to his tomb and found it empty. Not only this but the women had claimed to have seen angels who said that, in fact, Jesus was alive.

The apparent stranger rebukes the two disciples for their foolishness and begins to explain the scriptures to them, revealing how everything that has happened has been predicted previously and is the will of God. By the time they reach Emmaus, they are understandably tired and hungry with their intense conversation and walking. Jesus seems to want to go on ahead but, in true fellowship, the disciples urge him to stay for a meal. So Jesus, still a stranger to them, accepts their hospitality. It is here that we come to the climax of the story. Not only has Jesus had to listen to his disciples discussing his story without any knowledge of who he is, but he has had to give them a very long and comprehensive Bible lesson—at the end of which they still don't realise his identity.

Now, at the table, Jesus breaks the bread and blesses it, and the disciples recognise him at last. He is no stranger but their own Saviour. He has redeemed Israel after all. Then he disappears. Cleopas and his friend are so excited by the revelation that they don't even want to finish their meal. Instead, they hurry back to Jerusalem, overwhelmed by this extraordinary encounter, so that they can share the experience with their fellow disciples.

Before we make hasty judgments about these disciples and their initial inability to recognise Christ, we have to remember the many times when we, too, fail to notice him staring us in the face. We can be so busy looking for Christ that we fail to see that he is already here. Often, we come to understand aspects of our faith only over long periods of time. We are not quick thinkers; like most of the disciples, we don't grasp our faith easily. The obvious is very often obscure to us.

It seems likely, therefore, that only through the symbolic ritual of breaking bread could the two disciples recognise Jesus. This symbol, and not the preceding narrative, was the means by which Jesus was made present to them. This is why Lent is such a significant time for us to ponder these mysteries and to reflect on our faith journey in depth again. It is as well that Jesus is so patient!

If Good Friday represents the Old Testament and Easter Day represents the New, then Holy Saturday is the bridge of hope that connects the two. Jesus is the miracle of this bridge. So Easter Day is a new beginning without parallel, as if life were arising from death, the light emerging from the dark. A new love is waiting to embrace us when we joyfully believe in the risen Lord. When the stone is rolled away from our doubts, our fears and all that life has dealt us, when we are able to stand in the presence of our God, then we will have become what we were born to be.

The meal at Emmaus was both the last supper of Christ on earth and the first celebration of the risen Christ in the Eucharist. The thread of love is unbroken: Christ was, is and is to come at every point in our faith journey.

Spiritual exercise

❖ Imagine that Jesus is explaining the scriptures as you travel on the road to Emmaus with the two disciples. What would make your heart burn within you?

❖ Imagine you are watching Jesus bless the bread that evening and you suddenly recognise him as your Lord. What emotions do you feel?

❖ Reflect on the times when you receive the Eucharist at church. How does this passage enrich your faith?

❖ What does Jesus' resurrection mean in your life?

Prayer

Risen Lord,
may your loving power that shatters tombs
shatter any doubt in me.
My heart burns within me as the scriptures are fulfilled
and your blessings are revealed.
You are rising in my heart;
your grace is all I need.
Amen

Reflection

The resurrection makes everything possible because it is the ultimate victory over death. Give thanks today for the resurrection, God's miracle from beyond the grave. It is life completed and life renewed. It is an endless gift of his love and grace. Alleluia!

Mothers' Union

Mothers' Union is an international Christian charity that supports families worldwide.

We are a network of 4 million people in over 80 countries—women and men, single and married, parents and grandparents—who share one vision: to make manifest the love of God through the quality of our family and community relationships.

We serve Christ in our diverse communities through prayer, financial support and active work at grassroots level. We work directly with families through our parenting programme, prison visiting and contact centre, we campaign to challenge legislation that neglects the vulnerable and marginalised, and we are represented at the United Nations' Commission on the Status of Women.

If you would like to hear more about our faith in action and core global work, visit our website:

www.themothersunion.org

Alternatively, you can contact Marketing Unit, Mothers' Union, 24 Tufton Street, London, SW1P 3RB.

To give to the work of Mothers' Union supporting communities around the world and speaking out for family life, go to www.themothersunion.org/donate. You can also give over the phone, 020 7222 5533, or by writing to Mothers' Union at the address above.